Making Up The Numbers

Making Up The Numbers

The clubs that hoped to be giant killers

STUART SHEARD

Published by Drop Kick Books
www.dropkickbooks.co.uk

ISBN 978-0-9567444-2-5

British Library Cataloguing in Publications Data

A catalogue record for this book is available from the British Library

Book and cover design by Clare Brayshaw

Front cover photo – Steve O'Gorman, Heworth v Halifax 1988,
courtesy of The Press

Back cover photo – Goole 1937

Prepared and printed by:

York Publishing Services Ltd

64 Hallfield Road

Layerthorpe

York YO31 7ZQ

Tel: 01904 431213

Website: www.yps-publishing.co.uk

For Daniel – a rugby league book at last

I would like to thank my wife Mary for her endless patience and for editing the original document; Tony Collins for his wise advice; David Thorpe for helping me to access the Rugby League Archives, and last but not least Clare Brayshaw for her excellent work on the design and layout of this book.

Contents

Acknowledgements

Dave Johnson
Lee Robinson
Dennis Oaten
Bob Colgrave
Mark Chestney
The University of Huddersfield Archives
Phil Caplan
David Thorpe
Saddleworth Historical Society
David Gronow
Ken Sykes
Bernard Shooman
Daniel Sheard
Harry Edgar
Ian Golden
Curtis Johnstone
Craig Evans
Graham Morris
Mick McGowan

I am grateful to the following for giving me permission to use their photographs and documents to illustrate this book:

Robert Gate
Sig Kasatkin – RL Photos.com
Susan Butler
Dave Johnson
Craig Evans
David Thorpe
The Press
David Gronow
James Brammer – Huddersfield Giants
The Rugby League Archives
Heworth ARLFC
Matthew Richardson

Introduction

Prior to August 1895 and the breakaway that saw the formation of the Northern Union, the county cup in Yorkshire was the highlight of the rugby season for many players and spectators. Attendances at Yorkshire Cup Finals, and also in some of the earlier rounds, were often very impressive. The 1895 final between Brighouse Rangers and Morley was played at Headingley in front of 20,000 spectators. Brighouse won the Yorkshire Cup by defeating Morley by 16 points to 4, and the following season were one of the founder members of the Northern Union. Morley did not join the Northern Union although, if local folklore is to be believed, they had every intention of doing so. The story goes that the Morley officials who should have attended the meeting when the Northern Union was formed got rather distracted on their journey, visited a number of local hostelries, and never arrived in Huddersfield where the meeting was held. The story isn't true as Morley were not invited to the meeting at the George Hotel. However, in 1896 they were offered a place in the Yorkshire Senior Competition, but the club members voted not to accept the offer. Morley did join the Northern Union in 1897 but were not members of the Yorkshire Senior Competition and had to play friendlies for a season before joining the Yorkshire Second Competition. They took part in the Cup in 1898, receiving a walkover in the first round, before losing 11 points to nil away to Hull Kingston Rovers. The Morley Northern Union club managed to play in the following season, 1898/97, again in the Yorkshire Second Competition but then a combination of financial problems and a shortage of players caused the club to fold. Brighouse Rangers, the Cup winners in 1895, did join the Northern Union and played for eleven seasons before folding in 1906.

The kudos that came from being county cup winners was very important to the leading clubs and would certainly have led to the cup holders increasing their attendances as well as improving their ability to attract good players. It would have been no surprise, therefore, if there were discussions about organising a cup competition amongst the officials of the twenty two clubs that broke away from the Rugby Football Union to form the Northern Union. However, as the meeting to form the Northern Union was held on 29th August 1895, close to the start of a new season, the priority for the clubs involved would have been to organise league fixtures in order that the season could begin as soon as possible.

It is not clear from contemporary records exactly which clubs were leading the discussions that took place during the 1895/96 season regarding a Northern Union Cup, but it is unlikely that any of the member clubs would have opposed the plan to establish a cup competition. While the financial benefits from a successful cup run were obviously an important consideration for club treasurers, what was probably much more important was the status in the sport that came with being cup winners.

During that first Northern Union season, many of the discussions about the Northern Union Cup may well have focussed on how many clubs would take part. There were only twenty two senior Northern Union clubs in 1895, a figure that increased to thirty in 1896. Those numbers would have made it difficult for the Northern Union to establish a competition that was fair to all its members. Playing preliminary rounds in order to produce the sixteen clubs necessary for a first round draw could mean additional income, providing you drew attractive opponents. However, an extra round, or even two, would also mean a much more difficult route to the final.

This book discusses how the Northern Union and later the Rugby Football League (RFL) resolved the problem of constructing an annual cup competition when the number of professional clubs very rarely allowed there to be a straight knock out that was fair to all. The book will also consider the impact on the Cup of what we now call amateur or community clubs. Those are the clubs that in the early years of the Northern Union were called 'junior' clubs, the clubs that did not take part in the senior Northern Union competitions. In 1926 the Northern Rugby Football League, as it was then known, attempted to re-define junior clubs as amateur clubs. However, as with many of the innovations that have taken place in Rugby League, there were a number of people who felt the change of title for the clubs below senior level was not necessary. The reality was that by 1926 the majority of junior clubs were purely amateur. Using the term junior was also felt to be confusing; re-defining all the clubs below the main professional competition as amateur did seem a logical way forward. However, it probably wasn't until the British Amateur Rugby League Association (BARLA) was formed on 4th March 1973 that it was accepted by most people involved in the sport that all junior clubs should be called amateur.

During its first twenty years in existence, the Northern Union had a number of different competition formats. These included one league for all of its senior clubs, regional leagues based on geographical location and a two division structure based on playing ability. A number of the clubs that we know today as amateur or community clubs continued to pay some or all of their players. These clubs were members of the Northern Union but played league games in regional and district competitions and were honorary rather than full members. Some of these honorary members, Millom and Normanton being two good examples, played in the leagues that operated below the main Northern Union competition. They then joined the senior Northern Union clubs in their league competitions for a few seasons, before reverting back to junior status. Others such as Featherstone Rovers played in the junior leagues and the Cup for many seasons before joining the senior professional competition. For the purposes of this book, the clubs that I will be featuring are those that were not playing in the senior professional leagues when they took part in the Cup.

Over its one hundred and six years in existence, the Northern Union Cup that later became the Rugby League Challenge Cup has produced many highlights, mainly in the later stages, and often at venues like

Wembley, Headingley, Fartown and Central Park. However, in this book I hope to recognise some of the highlights and events that did not take place in front of large crowds at the leading venues. Rather, I intend to celebrate giant killers, unsung heroes and some rugby league games that were significant and important events in the local community where they took place.

Chapter 1

In the Beginning

The first ever Northern Union Cup competition took place at the end of the 1896/97 league season. The hope from Northern Union clubs and administrators presumably would be that this new competition would replicate the success of competitions like the Yorkshire Cup, both in terms of spectator interest and also in increased revenue for the Northern Union and the club's taking part.

The format of the new Cup will have been an important agenda item at Northern Union meetings during 1895/96. Although, the clubs and administrators will certainly have had many other important issues to confront as the first Northern Union season progressed, such as travel costs and the overall decline in attendances. Some clubs had suffered financially from playing fixtures against opponents that did not bring many supporters with them because of the distance they had to travel to the game. Reverting to a two league format with a Lancashire Senior Competition and a Yorkshire Senior Competition in 1896/97 must have been seen as a way of addressing some of the travel issues because it would ensure that there were more local derbies and fewer long journeys. The discussions about the format of the Cup competition must have continued at a pace because, at a meeting of the Northern Union in March 1896, the Northern Union Cup was officially announced. A committee was formed that was tasked with providing a cup and medals to play for. In June 1896 the Cup bye laws were issued. In the bye laws there was no mention of venues for the semi-finals and final or the way in which the gate receipts from those games would be divided up between the competing clubs and the Northern Union. It was widely assumed that the gate receipts from each game would be split three ways between the two clubs taking part and the Northern Union but there was also a view that as this was the first year of the new Cup all the income from the final should go to the Northern Union. The Northern Union did, in fact, keep all of the receipts from the first final, a decision that must have caused some financial problems for the two clubs that played in the game. If they did have to cover all the costs of their 'cup run' it is no wonder that the 1897 Cup finalists were a little disgruntled when in later years the Northern Union decided that each of the finalists should receive a financial reward for reaching that stage.

The draw for the first Northern Union Cup was made on 3rd September 1896 with the competition scheduled to begin on Saturday 20th March 1897. There were fifty two clubs taking part in this first ever national rugby competition, the type of national competition that wasn't allowed by the Rugby Football Union as they felt it would encourage professionalism. Unfortunately, in 1896 the Northern Union only had member clubs from Lancashire, Yorkshire and Cheshire and so the Cup couldn't really qualify as a national competition. However, because it had the largest geographical spread of clubs of any cup competition to date; it was nearest thing to a national competition rugby had ever seen.

There were forty clubs in the first round of the Cup, twenty five of which were members of either the Lancashire Senior Competition or the Yorkshire Senior Competition. Those twenty five clubs were joined by fifteen junior clubs, all honorary members of the Northern Union. There are some names familiar to us today amongst the fifteen juniors that played in the first round. Latchford, Waterhead and Eastmoor are all places that still have clubs taking part in the amateur/community game. The second round of the Cup which took place on 27th March 1897 saw the final five Northern Union clubs joined by six more junior clubs and Eastmoor who won their first round game against Oldham Juniors. It seems surprising that six junior clubs were given byes into the second round. Presumably all the clubs taking part in the cup competition were put into the hat for the draw and, once the first twenty ties had been

Action from Eastmoor v Loughborough 2013 Challenge Cup 1st Round

drawn, the rest of the clubs regardless of whether they were senior or junior were given a bye into the second round. Quite what clubs like Oldham, Huddersfield and Leigh, who all lost their first round games, thought about junior clubs being given a bye is not difficult to imagine. The loss of the opportunity of progress in the Cup and the possible loss of financial benefits from involvement in the later rounds will not have been good news for club committees. Although, as reaching the final in 1897 did not bring any financial reward, perhaps those senior clubs were in fact happy not to be taking part in the later stages of the new competition.

Round one of the Cup did not produce any shock results. In most cases the juniors were easily beaten by the seniors. In the eleven first round games won by the leading clubs, 549 points were scored against twenty two. The only clubs outside the senior competitions that put up respectable performances were Radcliffe against Wigan, Walkden against Hull and Rochdale St Clements against Leeds. The heavy defeats suffered by most of the junior clubs produced the reaction from some members of the press that the scores '*reduced the cup system to a farce*'. The hope for future years was that preliminary rounds would be introduced to reduce the number of junior clubs involved in games against senior opponents. Only one of the first round games was played at the ground of a junior club and it involved two junior clubs, Eastmoor and Oldham Juniors. The other junior club that was drawn at home was Runcorn Recreation who agreed to transfer their game against Leeds Parish Church to Crown Point, the Leeds club's home ground. Switching a cup tie to your opponents ground was allowed by the new Northern Union Cup rules, where a ground switch could take place if it was considered that the result was inevitable. Exactly how and who determined that the result of a game was inevitable is not clear. Presumably it was a decision made by the Northern Union based on the performance of the two clubs over the season. However, as the reason for switching the cup tie was usually because the senior club had offered their junior opponents a financial inducement, it does appear that 'lip service' was played to the rule regarding the inevitability of the result. The reality often was that once the junior club lost the advantage of playing on its own ground then the result probably was inevitable! This rule was one that was possibly adopted because switching grounds had happened, on occasions, in the Yorkshire Cup pre 1895. An example of ground switching took place in 1886 when Hull FC offered Salterhebble £100 to switch their Yorkshire cup tie. Hull had originally offered Salterhebble £75 but they refused and stuck out for £100. The rule that allows clubs to switch grounds has remained in existence since 1896 and was used many times over the coming years by senior clubs drawn away in the Cup who wished to play on their home ground and were prepared to compensate their opponents if they agreed to switch the game.

In the second round another all junior tie took place when Crompton beat Bradford Church Hill by 24 points to nil in front of 1,200 spectators. The senior Bradford club that had been drawn away to Swinton Church offered their opponents a financial guarantee to encourage them to transfer their second round game to Bradford, and with 5,000 spectators in attendance the seniors put 68 points past their luckless junior opponents. The Salford versus Werneth game was switched to Rochdale by mutual agreement, with Salford progressing to the next round after a 30 points to nil victory with 3,000 spectators present. Crompton's progress in the Cup came to a halt in the third round when they agreed to accept £60 compensation and expenses to switch their game against Halifax to the senior club's ground. Unfortunately for Halifax, the decision to offer the compensation to Crompton did not result in very much profit from the game. A gale force wind and sleet reduced the attendance, and as a result the income from the gate did not leave a big margin for the home club. The one positive note for Halifax was that they had a comfortable passage into the next round. The senior club's backs proved too strong for Crompton, with six tries and seven goals producing a winning margin of 50 points to nil.

Eastmoor, the only junior club that took part in the 1897 competition to also featured in the 2013 Challenge Cup, came close to reaching the third round when they had a 3-3 draw in their second round game at home to senior club Stockport. Both sides were evenly matched. However, the strong wind was a factor in Eastmoor's favour, as it was said in the match report to have '*nullified Stockport's open play*'. After a scoreless opening forty minutes, Eastmoor struck first with an unconverted try to which Stockport replied with an unconverted try close to the end of the game to force the replay. Unfortunately, the following Wednesday evening, when the replayed game took place at Stockport in front of 1,000 spectators, Eastmoor were beaten by 28 points to 8. The match report in the Yorkshire Post said that '*Eastmoor played grandly and showed good football*'. Eastmoor's performance against Stockport was very creditable as the Lancashire Senior Competition club had finished the league season in fifth place with fourteen wins from twenty six games. Had Eastmoor taken their opportunities in the first game between the clubs, perhaps they could have claimed the proud title of the first rugby league giant killers.

Crompton's defeat in the third round ended the junior club involvement in the Cup and the senior's were left to fight out the later stages. The final between Batley and St Helens was held at Headingley. The game was won by Batley by 10 points to 3 with 13,492 spectators present, a significant decrease in attendance when compared with the 1895 Yorkshire Cup Final played at the same venue. The decreased attendance may have confirmed the view of the Northern Union administrators that they were right to split the senior clubs into two regional leagues. The distance and cost of travel that reduced the attendance when clubs from either side of the Pennines played each other seemed borne out by the Cup Final attendance. However, there could have been other factors that led to the attendance being smaller than for the 1895 Yorkshire Cup Final. Batley were not one of the best supported Yorkshire clubs, as they were based in a small town rather than one of the big cities such as Bradford or Leeds. The Northern Union Cup was also a new competition played at the end of the season and perhaps Northern Union supporters had decided that they had seen enough rugby during the league season. Another factor in some of the poor attendances, particularly in the early rounds, may have been the doubling of the admission price for all the cup ties and the fact that there were so many mismatches in the early rounds. The decision to double the admission price was not commented on when a number of clubs recorded smaller than expected attendances. However, the price of admission must have been a factor in the reduced interest in Cup matches because, when the same opponents had met in the earlier league season, those games had attracted much bigger crowds.

Despite the mismatches and attendance issues at some games, the Cup was here to stay and Batley, who reached the final again in 1901, went down in rugby league history as the first ever winners.

Chapter 2

The age of the Giant Killers

Over the next twelve years the Northern Union made a number of changes to the format of the Cup competition. Some of them were an attempt to address the concerns raised in 1897 regarding mismatches. Other changes were made because as the number of clubs playing Northern Union increased, different formats had to be put into place in order to reach the 'magic number' of sixty four. This number was required in the draw for the first round in order for the knockout competition to eventually produce two finalists. The Northern Union addressed the issue of how to get to the 'magic numbers' of sixty four and then in later years thirty two clubs in the first round draw by playing qualifying rounds, preliminary rounds, and also by seeding and regionalising the qualifying rounds.

The changes to the format of the Cup were gradually introduced over the next few years. But in 1898 there were no changes to the format. Twenty eight junior clubs went into the draw for the first round, along with the thirty senior clubs that were playing fixtures in the new regional league structure. Fourteen of the senior clubs were in the Lancashire Senior Competition and sixteen in the Yorkshire Senior Competition. The second year of the Cup saw the first conceded games with four junior clubs Abbey Hills, Lostock Gralem, Morley and Radcliffe all receiving byes into the second round after their junior opponents scratched. For some junior clubs, the issue of travel costs to a game where there was unlikely to be an attendance large enough to cover the costs that both clubs would have incurred could have been the main reason for some of the juniors deciding to withdraw.

In the first round of the 1898 competition there were far fewer one sided games than in the previous season with only the 46 points to nil Hull Kingston Rovers versus Hull Marlborough tie standing out as a mismatch. Unfortunately, there were no giant killers but Salford, who finished the Lancashire Senior Competition season in fourth place, struggled to beat Millom by 9 points to 2 while Hunslet who finished top of the Yorkshire Senior Competition only managed to beat Lancaster by 8 points to 3. Three junior clubs Altringham, Barton and Fleetwood got through to the third round by beating junior opposition in the second round. In the third round, Barton at home to Bramley came closest to causing an upset only losing by 9 points to 3. There were 3,000 spectators at Barton, on the 19th March 1898, and it was reported in the Yorkshire Post that the junior club were always in the contest. Their backs were described in the match report as having '*a splendid passing game*'. The ability to kick goals was the difference between the two teams. Two first half dropped goals added to the conversion to Bramley's only try proving decisive. In the other third round games, Altringham lost to Salford by 16 points to nil and Fleetwood lost to Hull Kingston Rovers by 31 points to nil.

In 1899 the Northern Union had decided that no more than sixty four clubs would be required in the first round and so the competition changed from being open to all to having qualifying rounds for junior clubs. The first giant killers appear in the 1899 competition when twenty six junior clubs made up the numbers but unfortunately there were more mismatches than had occurred the previous season, prompting the following comment that appeared in the press: '*Many of the ties were go-as-you-please victories for the winning team. For instance Runcorn (18 tries and 8 goals -70) Oldham (17 tries and 6 goals -63), Broughton Rangers (13 tries and 10 goals -59), Salford (15 tries and 9 goals -63), Swinton (8 tries and 8 goals -40),Batley (10 tries and 4 goals -38) and Widnes (12 tries and 6 goals -48), the latter fielding ten 'A' team men against Fleetwood, had to take part in matches that were little better than a farce. These inequalities suggest the necessity for still further extending the qualifying stage of the competition so that clubs with serious responsibilities may not have to waste their time taking part in hack* games'. Comments and scores like the ones listed in the quote above provided more ammunition for those people within the Northern Union who wished to reduce even further the number of junior clubs taking part in the Cup. However, I am sure that Normanton's second round 7 points to 2 victory over senior club Holbeck will have caused some concerns for the other senior clubs languishing at the lower end of the league tables. Holbeck had finished the Yorkshire Senior Competition season in 13th place but had managed to win ten games the same number as Castleford, the club above them, and more than Bramley, Liversedge and Heckmondwike the three clubs below them. The draw hadn't matched Castleford, Bramley, Liversedge, Heckmondwike or Morecambe the bottom club in the Lancashire Senior Competition against junior opposition but if it had there may well have been more giant killing acts.

Normanton's second round tie with Holbeck was played at Holroyd's Paddock in front of a very vociferous home crowd. Normanton had been in poor form in the league and were not expected to beat Holbeck, but a strong first half performance by the home team saw them take a 7 points to nil half time lead. In the second half, Holbeck could not breech the Normanton defence, with their only points coming from a penalty. In the third round Normanton took 1,500 spectators with them to Fartown to face Huddersfield, but despite a courageous display they were defeated by their senior opponents by 23 points to 2.

Normanton's 1899 Cup campaign was the prelude to a period when any club visiting the town was guaranteed a tough encounter. It was a junior club that very few senior outfits will have relished drawing in the Cup. Normanton was one of the strong junior clubs that managed to make the step up to the senior level joining the Yorkshire Senior Competition in 1901 before playing for four seasons as a member of the Northern Union second division. Millom was another club, still in existence today and like Normanton playing fixtures in the National Conference League, that had a spell from 1899 until 1906 first in the Lancashire Senior Competition and then in the second division of the Northern Union. There are other clubs still involved in the professional game at the present time, such as Barrow and Featherstone Rovers who played as junior clubs only meeting senior opposition when they were drawn against them in the Cup. For some junior clubs the fact that they were already paying some of their players must have made the step up to the senior ranks much easier.

Goole played in the first round for the first time in 1899 and were drawn at home to Oldham and, as expected, were offered an incentive by the senior club to switch the tie. Goole played on Victoria Pleasure Grounds, a facility more than capable of hosting the tie. However, Goole were not having a very good season in the Yorkshire Second Competition and the expected attendance would probably not have covered costs. Therefore, when Oldham offered Goole £50 to switch the tie it was gratefully accepted. Goole travelled by train for a game that produced seventeen Oldham tries and some very negative comments in the match reports, one in particular describing the game as '*a farce*'.

Over the next few years there were other changes to the format of the Cup, the first of which happened in 1904 when an intermediate round was played. This was seen as the final preliminary round before the competition proper began. The seventeen Northern Union second division clubs were joined by the eleven junior clubs that had progressed from the earlier qualifying rounds. This gave the fourteen intermediate round winners an opportunity to play against one of the eighteen first division clubs that entered the Cup at the first round stage.

Normanton continued their giant killing exploits in 1900 when, in front of 5,000 spectators and again at Holroyd's Paddock, they beat a weakened Leeds team by 5 points to nil. This game and the excellent local support must have helped to persuade the Normanton committee that the town could sustain a senior club. As Leeds had finished next to bottom of the Yorkshire Senior Competition and had only picked up seven wins all season, they must have made the short journey to Normanton expecting the worst. Normanton's progress in the Cup came to halt in the second round when they again attracted over 5,000 spectators for the tie against Batley but lost by 3 points to nil. Normanton matched Batley in the forwards but their backs lacked the skill to breakdown the Batley defence.

Goole appeared in the first round again in 1900 and this time staged the tie against Heckmondwike on their home ground. Heckmondwike had finished bottom of the Yorkshire Senior Competition the previous season, dropped out of the professional ranks, and were now operating as a junior club. Because of their opponent's greater experience, Goole were not expected to be able to match them, even on their own ground. However, an inspired display described in the Goole Times as '*the best they had played all season*' saw them win by 8 points to 6. Goole's reward was a trip to Warrington where unfortunately they were easily beaten by 44 points to 8.

In the 1901 Cup, and just prior to joining the Yorkshire Senior Competition, Normanton were again involved in a very closely fought first round tie, losing by 3 points to 2 at Yorkshire Senior Competition strugglers Liversedge. The giant killers this year were the Merseyside club Birkenhead Wanderers. In the first round they beat Millom by 2 points to nil before meeting Ossett, another junior club, in the second round. The teams drew 5-5 at Ossett, but in the replay Birkenhead ran out comfortable winners by 20 points to 2. In the third round Birkenhead, who joined the Lancashire Senior Competition the following year, met their match losing by 10 points to 2 at home to Widnes. Goole also came close to progressing to the second round when they played St Helens at home. The 12 points to 2 defeat on a very heavy pitch did not really reflect how close the game was.

Over the first four years of the Cup the number of junior clubs from Cumbria had increased. In 1902 Askham, Wath Brow, Penrith and Kendal joined clubs such as Whitehaven Recreation, Aspatria and Maryport who had played in previous seasons. The journey to and from Cumbria at the turn of the Twentieth Century must have been a daunting and expensive one. The cost of travel was probably what caused Workington to concede their first round game at Bradford junior club Idle. The gate at Idle, if the tie had taken place, would probably not have covered the home club's costs let alone the cost of Workington's travel to Yorkshire. However, Idle were destined to play Cumbrian opposition in 1902 as they drew Workington's near neighbours

Whitehaven Recreation in round two. The game in Bradford was a 5-5 draw which meant that Idle had to travel to the Cumbrian coast for the replay, losing by 6 points to 3. Whitehaven Recreation's Cup run ended in the third round when they lost at Swinton by 34 points to nil. Bradford juniors Windhill were the giant killers in 1902 after beating Millom by 5 points to nil. The Cumbrians were adjusting well to life in the Lancashire Senior Competition and so losing to a junior club was unexpected. Windhill conceded home advantage in the second round and were easily beaten by Leeds. Two of the other Cumbrian clubs provided stern opposition for the senior outfits they played at home. Askham lost 3 points to nil to Widnes while Lancashire Senior Competition club Rochdale Hornets just managed to beat Aspatria by 4 points to 2. The other close games in the first round in 1902 saw Outwood Church draw 5-5 with Morecambe before losing the replay by 15 points to nil and Otley losing by 5 points to nil at home to Leeds. Ossett, who beat Seaton by 5 points to 2 and Todmorden by 15 points to 2 to reach the third round, lost by 7 points to 4 at Heckmondwike with over 2,000 spectators in attendance.

By 1903 the geographical spread of the Cup with clubs in the draw from Cumbria, Cheshire, Lancashire, Yorkshire and the North East began to have an impact on some of the junior clubs taking part. Three clubs in the first round draw, Penrith United, Goole and Wallsend all disbanded while Altringham and Todmorden both scratched, the latter citing lack of funds as the reason. Although no results are recorded it is clear that there had been a number of preliminary or qualifying rounds in 1903 as some of the regular entrants such as Eastmoor, Askham and Aspatria were not involved in the first round which had sixty four clubs in the draw. There were no giant killers in 1903 but Idle came very close to defeating their senior neighbours Manningham, drawing 0-0 before losing the replay by 12 points to nil. Maryport, who had a bye in the first round, made it through to the third round by beating Parton 5 points to nil in the second round after a replay. In the third round, Maryport gave a good account of themselves at first division Runcorn before losing 17 points to 3.

In 1904, two qualifying rounds took place on the 6th and 13th February with the qualifiers joining the seventeen second division clubs in the intermediate round. The giant killers were Parton who beat second division Millom by 8 points to 7 before losing to Broughton Rangers 26 points to nil in the first round. Parton gave up ground advantage playing the tie at Broughton in return for a £40 guarantee. The other junior club that made it through to the first round was Brookland Rovers who beat near neighbours Maryport 2 points to nil before they also conceded home advantage to Salford in exchange for a guaranteed £50. Brookland lost the game at Salford by 57 points to nil. I am sure that if Brookland Rovers and perhaps Parton had staged the cup ties on their own ground the score could have been much closer. Brookland Rovers would certainly have provided a much sterner test at home to first division Salford who, at the time, were one of the leading clubs in the Northern Union. The Lancastrians would surely not have relished the long trip to Cumbria to face one of the top junior clubs in the game in front of their partisan supporters. Conceding home advantage in return for a financial reward is a recurring theme in this story of the Cup and one that I will explore further.

There were no giant killing acts in 1905 although Chadderton did come very close in their intermediate round game losing by 2 points to nil at second division Rochdale Hornets. Brookland Rovers again reached the first round but in unusual circumstances. They lost their intermediate round tie against local rivals Maryport by 10 points to 5 but then appealed to the Northern Union for the game to be replayed because they claimed that Maryport had played an ineligible player. Their appeal was upheld and in the replay Brookland Rovers scraped home by 2 points to nil. In the first round Brookland Rovers again conceded home advantage to Hull Kingston Rovers and were heavily beaten 73 points to 5 in front of 4,000 spectators. All the other junior clubs that played in the first round were beaten by senior opposition. Leigh Shamrocks lost 52 points to nil at Hull; Parton went down 22 points to 3 at Hunslet, while Ossett put up a good fight at first division Leeds before losing by 20 points to nil in front of 9,000 spectators.

Featherstone Rovers were the 1906 giant killers. The junior club began its Cup campaign in the first qualifying round on 25th November 1905 beating Knottingley and then Woolley Colliery, Otley and Brookland Rovers on the way to a second round clash with Widnes at home, which they won by 23 points to 2. The result was described in the Athletic News as the sensation of the second round. The game attracted Featherstone's biggest crowd of the year and the match report described it as a *'rout'*. Featherstone Rovers were, therefore, very confident when they visited Keighley in the third round. Unfortunately, their progress in the Cup was halted at Keighley, where they lost by 3 points to nil. Although Featherstone's big tough forwards took some handling, Keighley's backs were described as far stronger than Featherstone's and the home club deserved the win. Featherstone, despite this successful Cup run, did not appear in the first round again until 1913 and continued as a junior club until 1921 when they joined the Northern Union as full members. Widnes, the club that Featherstone defeated in the second round, had been fortunate to reach that stage. In their first round match against Victoria Rangers, played in front of 6,000 spectators at the Park Avenue ground in Bradford, neither club could get the upper hand a 0-0 draw being the result. In the replay that attracted only 500 spectators Widnes eventually ran out winners by 8 points to 3. In the second half of the game the Victoria Rangers players had threatened to walk off after Widnes scored a disputed close range try. They were persuaded to stay on the field but were not able score the necessary points required to take them into the next round. Egerton were the other junior club to reach the second round following a 9 points to nil victory over Leigh Shamrocks. The Manchester based club then lost 38 points to 5 at neighbours Salford.

Bramley had a disastrous 1906/07 season only managing to win one game of the twenty they played. It was, therefore, no surprise when Leeds juniors Saville Green became giant killers by beating them in the intermediate round by 10 points to nil.

Newington Rovers from Hull was one of another two clubs that came close to providing an upset in 1907. In the intermediate round they drew twice with York before losing a second replay by 14 points to 5. Workington was the other junior club that was close to becoming giant killers. They drew 3-3 with Wakefield Trinity in a game where only poor finishing by the Cumbrians gave Trinity an opportunity for another 'bite of the cherry'. In the replay, in Yorkshire, Wakefield won by 16 points to 5.Whitehaven Recreation did reach the second round by beating giant killers Saville Green by 10 points to nil only to lose to Keighley by 14 points to nil. Keighley had attempted to persuade Whitehaven to switch the tie, but their offer was refused. Keighley travelled to Cumbria on the Friday evening before the game, a recognition that they were taking their junior opponents very seriously. Keighley held a 6 points to nil half time lead and in the second half their greater experience proved decisive. The tie attracted 2,000 spectators.

In 1908 Whitehaven Recreation did become giant killers, beating St Helens by 13 points to 8 in front of over 2,000 enthusiastic Cumbrians. St Helens were really struggling in the 1907/08 Northern Union season and finished in twenty fifth place in a league of twenty seven. The trip to face Whitehaven Recreation probably produced the result that most observers of the sport expected. Whitehaven's opponents in the second round were Merthyr Tydfil, but the long trip to South Wales proved too much for the Cumbrians and they lost 33 points to 5. Merthyr had reached the second round by beating Beverley away by 15 points to 3 in front of a very small attendance that provided the Welsh club with only £3 16s 6d as their share of the gate. Unfortunately Beverley, were unwilling to pay Merthyr their share and were suspended from all competitions until the money was paid. Wigan Highfield, another club that later joined the senior ranks, nearly provided an upset in their first round game with a 3-3 draw against Bramley in front of 2,500 spectators but then lost the replay by 8 points to 6.

1909 was a significant year for the Challenge Cup as it was the last time for many years that a junior club would perform a giant killing act. Beverley was the club that achieved that feat by beating Ebbw Vale at home. Beverley were able to enter the 1909 Cup as their suspension was lifted towards the end of the 1907/08 season after they finally paid

Merthyr Tydfil their share of the gate for the 1908 cup tie. The Beverley club known locally as the Beavers were unbeaten leaders of the East Riding League, and very confident of beating Ebbw Vale. Playing uphill in the first half, Beverley's forwards managed to match their much heavier opponents and with the half time score at 2-2 the juniors began the second half full of confidence. Their victory was sealed when Fred Ward scored a try and then dropped a goal from close to the half way line. Over 2,000 spectators witnessed the giant killing act; an event that few of them will have realised would not be repeated in their lifetime. Beverley played at Halifax in the second round, and although they were heavily beaten by 53 points to 2, will have benefitted financially from a 5,546 attendance that produced gate receipts of £113.

Ebbw Vale 1908/09

The age of the giant killers was over and although there were many very close games in future years it would be a long time before any junior clubs managed to equal the Cup exploits of Beverley, Birkenhead Wanderers, Featherstone Rovers, Normanton, Parton, Whitehaven Recreation, Windhill and Saville Green.

Chapter 3

The Gap Begins to Widen

From 1910 on the number of junior clubs taking part in the first round of the Cup decreased as the number of qualifying rounds increased. The concerns expressed by clubs and the newspaper commentators regarding some of the mismatches in the early rounds had been acted upon by the Northern Union. Up to five qualifying rounds were played every season, often regionalised, with junior clubs playing a number of the early qualifying rounds against clubs from their own district. In the early qualifying rounds, the lack of travel issues because of the number of local derbies was obviously intended to reduce costs, one of the reasons that junior clubs often used for conceding a game and withdrawing from the Cup. The number of clubs entering reflected the fact that the juniors were obviously still keen to be involved in a competition that could enhance their reputation and also bring financial rewards. However, in many cases where clubs received financial inducements from senior opponents to concede home advantage, the financial rewards were often considered much more important than an enhanced reputation.

When York Irish National League were drawn at home to Salford in the first round in 1910 an offer of £37 10s was sufficient to convince them to switch the game. Salford even offered to increase the compensation to £50 if the gate exceeded £100, although whether York INL actually received £50 is not clear as the gate at Salford is not recorded. What is recorded is the 64 points to nil trouncing that INL received a result that certainly did not enhance their reputation. The 1910 Cup did not produce any really close games when junior and senior clubs met. The

10 points to 23 defeat suffered by Purston White Horse at home to Halifax, in front 3,000 spectators, was the closest any of the junior clubs came to causing an upset. Purston were one of the stronger junior clubs as they were playing against many senior clubs 'A' teams as members of the Northern Union Combination.

In 1911 a very unusual event took place in one of the first round games involving a junior club. Broughton Moor, from Cumbria, were playing senior club Runcorn in terrible weather conditions. Heavy rain and gale force winds at Broughton Moor's exposed hill top ground had made it very difficult for both players and spectators. Runcorn established a healthy 23 points to 6 lead when, with twenty minutes left to play Broughton Moor decided to withdraw from the game! The reason given for the withdrawal was that, in the view of the Broughton players, Runcorn had won and there was no point in prolonging the ordeal for either players or spectators. There were some competitive ties in 1911. Pemberton, the Wigan junior club that was also a member of the Northern Union Combination, had a close game at home to Bradford Northern, losing by 4 points to 12 in a tie that attracted an attendance of 1,500 and receipts of £30. In the first half, with the strong wind at their backs, Bradford took a 10 points to 2 half time lead. However, in the second half, described in the Yorkshire Post match report as '*uninteresting*', neither team was able put a meaningful attack together and two penalty goals, one from either side, meant that Bradford progressed to the next round. However, this was not the closest result involving a junior club in 1911. Following their withdrawal from the senior ranks at the end of the 1905/06 season, Normanton re-appeared in 1911 as Normanton St John's and came within four points of beating Broughton Rangers. They lost at home by 6 points to 10 to the club that went on to win the Northern Union Cup that year. This was no mean feat and clearly marked Normanton St John's down as dangerous opponents for any club drawn away to them. In fact had Normanton been able to convert the two tries they scored plus the other penalty chances they had, they may well have become giant killers again. The difficulty of the task for any club drawn at Normanton was emphasised the following year when they entertained Warrington at their Mopsey Garth ground and drew 6 -6. Normanton had marched impressively through the qualifying rounds and after their heroics in the previous year could obviously be expected, as usual, to provide tough opposition to any club they played at home. The Normanton team was described in the Wakefield Express report on the tie as '*composed of a body of youths remarkable for their litheness and mobility and player for player they would weigh a stone less than their opponents*'. This, the match reporter believed, gave Normanton an advantage on the sticky and sloping Mopsey Garth pitch. The other advantage attributed to Normanton was that the majority of their players arrived at the game having done a full day's work at the pit. The reporter suggested that '*this natural mode of training appeared to have every man in the fittest possible condition*'. This was a remarkable statement, and in strong contrast to views today about the amount of rest required by modern day players before they take to the field. Normanton certainly pushed home their perceived advantages and restricted Warrington to only two sustained passing movements throughout the eighty minutes, both of which led to unconverted tries. The draw was sealed by Normanton's centre, Fred Goodfellow. The former Holbeck player kicked a penalty in the 78th minute. Unfortunately, Normanton's visit to Warrington for the replay on the following Monday did not end so happily as they lost by 75 points to nil. Playing at home in the first game had obviously given Normanton a significant advantage and perhaps this was a lesson that some other junior clubs should have taken on board before they decided to accept the financial inducements offered to switch a cup tie to their opponents ground. Normanton, despite being a strong junior club, were not really expected to trouble their more senior opponents. The team was described by some contemporary commentators as '*only small potatoes*'! The gap in skill, fitness and physique between senior and junior clubs was perceived to have widened, and with the last giant killing act having taken place three years earlier, the senior clubs no doubt felt very confident when they went into a Cup game against a junior club. The other significant tie in 1912 saw Keighley overcome the long trip to Cumbria and defeat former senior outfit Millom by 11 points to nil. In earlier years, the trip to the North West coast to face a tough Cumbrian team would have been a daunting prospect for many of the less successful senior clubs. Keighley had struggled during the 1911/12 league season and were not really in control of the game until the middle of the second half but, once they had taken control, they had too much skill and experience for their junior opponents.

Bradford Northern did not have any problems in 1913 when they faced Pemberton again in the first round, winning the tie by 33 points to 4. The two relatively close results involved Yorkshire based clubs. Normanton St John's again met senior opponents at Mopsey Garth. Oldham were attractive visitors as 5,000 spectators surrounded the pitch for what the locals hoped would be another good performance from their heroes. Normanton matched their senior opponents in the forwards but Oldham had too much skill and experience in their backline and won the tie by 17 points to 4. After this game it would be nearly forty years and two World Wars later before a Normanton club appeared again in the Challenge Cup first round proper. Elland was the other Yorkshire junior club involved in a tight game with senior opponents after they lost by 15 points to 2 against Wakefield Trinity. Elland had been drawn at home and managed to attract an estimated attendance of 5,000 to a game that produced receipts of £143. In the match report Elland were described as playing in *'a very stubborn manner'*. The junior club were very strong in the forwards but couldn't match Wakefield in the backs. Wakefield's best player was Tommy Poynton, their England International, who scored two second half tries to seal the win.

The 1914 competition produced a first round result that must have confirmed the views of many people at the time that the gap between senior and junior clubs was widening to the extent that many of the first round games involving junior clubs were meaningless events. Swinton Park was the unfortunate junior club to have drawn Huddersfield in the first round. Huddersfield was one of the outstanding teams of the era, and in wingman Albert Rosenfeld they had one of best finishers in the history of the game. The eighty tries he scored in the 1913/14 is a rugby league record that will probably never be broken. Swinton Park were drawn at home but decided to switch the game to Huddersfield's Fartown ground which at least meant that they gained financially. Rosenfeld and company ran riot scoring twenty seven tries in their 119 points to 2 victory. At one point in the second half, the 6,702 spectators must have thought that they might see two hundred points scored by Huddersfield, as every time the home team had the ball they crossed the Swinton Park line with very little difficulty. Swinton Park were described in the match report as '*feeble opponents*'. Major Holland, the Huddersfield full back, kicked nineteen goals and would have probably kicked more had he not been relieved of the kicking duties for some of the second half tries. A 62 points to nil victory by Hull Kingston Rovers over Millom, and a 45 points to nil home win by York against Cumbrian club Glasson Rangers, added to the widely held view that despite increasing the number of qualifying rounds the Northern Union Cup still had too many one sided ties.

Major Holland – Huddersfield

This chapter has focussed on the widening of the gap between junior and senior clubs, and the results in 1914 seemed to confirm that the gap was indeed widening. The results in 1915 must have therefore appeared to contradict the widening gap theory until you take into account the fact that the first round was played during the ravages of the First World War. The War that began in August 1914 had a massive impact on sport at all levels. The Northern Union had decided to continue with its league and cup competitions, despite the outbreak of hostilities but, with so many young men volunteering to fight, every club must have lost some of its regular players. The results in 1915 were therefore probably affected by the War, with Keighley's 8 points to 5 victory over

Askham on a very muddy Lawkholme Lane pitch and Swinton's 2 point win at Wigan Highfield more to do with the strength of the teams the senior clubs fielded rather than a narrowing of the gap back to pre-1909 days. All the clubs had to rely on servicemen being given leave in order to play. Fielding your best team every week, during wartime, would have been very difficult. However, despite the impact of the War there were still no giant killing acts. The Cup and formal league structures were suspended in 1915 because of a Government ban on competitive sport and so there were no further opportunities for the War to have an impact on results. The Northern Union Championship and the Cup re-started in the 1919/20 season.

Chapter 4

Adults, Apostles and Dabs

Rugby league at junior and amateur level has always been blessed with unusual club names, probably none more unusual than some of the clubs featured in this chapter which deals with the period from 1920 until the beginning of the Second World War.

In this inter-war period the gap in skills, fitness and physique between junior and senior clubs continued to widen so that the possibility of giant killing acts became less and less likely. As is often the case in knockout competitions, a lot of what happens in games in the early rounds depends on the luck of the draw. In 1913, Swinton Park had the misfortune to draw Huddersfield, one of the outstanding teams of the period. Had Swinton Park drawn one of the weaker senior clubs they may well been part of a much more competitive tie, but perhaps not gained as much financially. Junior clubs continued to enter the qualifying rounds in large numbers, most of them probably hoping to progress to the first round proper and draw a top senior club. Had junior clubs given up on the idea of beating senior opposition, or was the Cup seen as means of sealing your future financially if you reached the first round proper? This question is one that could have been asked every year that the Challenge Cup has been played and it is probably still a relevant question to ask even today.

Junior clubs just making up the numbers became even more obvious in the period between the Wars. Seven juniors were involved in the first round proper in 1920, a figure that fluctuated depending on how many senior clubs were playing in the Championship. Only two junior clubs were included in the first round in the mid-1930s, even though over one hundred clubs had taken part in five rounds of the qualifying competition. When the number of senior clubs decreased, the number of junior clubs increased, ensuring that the 'magic number' of thirty two was always achieved. The Northern Union, which became the Northern Rugby Football League in 1922, used different systems nearly every year to decide which clubs would qualify for the first round proper. In some years it was a club from one of the regional qualifying competitions that were usually played in districts. In other years a Lancashire and a Yorkshire representative would be allowed to take part, with the qualifying rounds appearing to be a separate competition. The prize for winning these rounds was an opportunity to play against senior opposition. It must have been very frustrating for some ambitious junior clubs who wanted the opportunity to test themselves against senior opponents, when they realised that in the season they were at their strongest only two junior clubs were required in the first round proper, when in previous seasons up to five had taken part. It was obviously much more difficult to qualify to face the 'big boys' when there was room for only two junior clubs in the first round draw.

The 1919/1920 competition, the first after the end of World War One had, as mentioned earlier, seven junior clubs in the first round facing senior opponents. One of the seven was Featherstone Rovers and another was Wigan Highfield, two of the junior clubs that joined the Championship in the 1920s. There were some very one sided games in the 1920 Challenge Cup. Halifax beat Brookland Rovers 55 points to nil, Hull easily accounted for BOCM winning by 75 points to nil, while Leeds had little difficulty against Cumbrian opponents beating Millom by 44 points to nil at Headingley. 1920 saw the first and only appearance in the first round proper of Healey Street Adults. This Oldham based club were drawn against Wigan, at Central Park, a very difficult proposition for any junior outfit particularly as Wigan took the tie very seriously and fielded a nearly full strength team. Healey Street also had a strong team on duty including Thomas Steele who, as a Sergeant in the 1st Battalion Seaforth Highlanders, had received the Victoria Cross

Healey Street Adults,
Thomas Steele VC is second from the left on the back row

in 1917 for conspicuous bravery and devotion to duty. Steele played on the right wing in a team that struggled from the first whistle. Put on the defensive from the kick off, Healey Street held out for the opening minutes of the game with some keen tackling, but once Wigan scored Healey Street could not contain their senior opponents and seven more tries followed to give a half time score of 36 points to 3. Wigan found it easy to add further tries in the second half running out 64 points to 3 winners. The consolation for Healey Street was the attendance of 5,000, which meant that their share of the gate was over £100. Thomas Steele played his part in the game, particularly in defence. In its match report the Wigan Observer mentioned Steele in the description of the period shortly after half time as follows: '*The visitors* (Healey Street Adults) *had the benefit of the strong sun at their backs in resuming and managed to hold the home attack for nearly ten minutes, chiefly by the efforts of Steele and Radford.*' It is remarkable, considering the serious injuries that Thomas Steele received in Mesopotamia, where he won the Victoria Cross, that he was able to play competitive rugby only three years later. Thomas Steele signed for Broughton Rangers on the 2nd March 1922 and played at centre in two first team games, one against Rochdale on 14th April 1922, and the other against Barrow on the 22nd April 1922. He was also on the playing register for Broughton Rangers the following season but did not make any further first team appearances.

Over the next four years, three junior clubs that all proved themselves in the Cup joined the senior ranks. Featherstone Rovers, who were involved in a close game with Dewsbury in the second round in 1921, joined the 'big boys' in September 1921. Wigan Highfield, who drew their 1922 first round game with Widnes before losing the replay by 5 points to 4, joined in September 1922. Castleford, who joined the senior ranks in September 1926, made four consecutive appearances in the first round before they joined. In 1923 against Salford they defended well but did not really threaten the senior club's try line. The ties against mid table teams Hull Kingston Rovers in 1924, and Hunslet in 1925, both resulted in fairly easy victories to the senior clubs, 24 points to 2 in 1924 and 25 points to nil in 1925. However, when Castleford played St Helens Recreation, in 1926, the narrow 18 points to 12 win by the senior club perhaps indicated that Castleford had made progress on the field and could be confident of surviving in the Championship. The cup tie performances of the three clubs against senior opposition must obviously have helped to convince the rest of the Championship that they were viable additions. All three clubs struggled initially but two of the three, Featherstone Rovers and Castleford, are still important parts of the rugby league scene today. In 1921, Askham lost by 7 points to 2 at home to Bradford, and in 1922 lost 15 points to nil, in a second round game at Keighley. Askham was the only junior club to really give senior opponents a close game in the early 1920s. Scores like the 54 points to 2 beating that Rochdale Hornets gave Broughton Moor, and the 73 points Wardley conceded against St Helens, continued to confirm that there was a gap in skill and experience between the junior and senior clubs and that it was probably getting wider.

It was 1925 when the Apostles appeared! The Twelve Apostles was the name of a Leigh junior club that played Leeds at Headingley losing by 27 points to nil. The Twelve Apostles appeared again in 1928 when

Twelve Apostles v Bradford 1928

they lost by 17 points to nil against Bradford Northern. This was a game described in the match report in the Yorkshire Post as a '*mud lark*'. It was also reported that Bradford had underestimated their opponents who defended well but struggled in attack. Both performances were an indication of the strength of the junior game in Leigh. Unfortunately, the 1925 Challenge Cup also saw another junior club concede more than 100 points. Flimby and Fothergill from Cumbria played Wigan at Central Park and lost the tie by 116 points to nil. Flimby and Fothergill arrived in the first round, as the Wigan Observer stated, '*with a very fine reputation*'. Flimby and Fothergill were Cumberland Champions and had won a number of cups. This was possibly one of the reasons for the £525 gate receipts from the game which meant that, despite the defeat, Flimby and Fothergill will have been well rewarded financially for their visit to Lancashire. As well as the score, the game was also

Jim Sullivan – Wigan

notable for the twenty two goals kicked by Jim Sullivan, the legendary Wigan full back. This was a record number of goals in a match and one of the rugby league records that still stands today.

In the 1926 first round an event took place that was becoming increasingly rare, a junior club played host to a senior club on their own ground. Hensingham, from Cumbria, had drawn Huddersfield at home and, as was usual in these cases, Huddersfield offered Hensingham compensation if they were prepared to switch the game. Hensingham refused the initial offer and surprisingly the senior club decided not to increase it and instead travelled to Cumbria. It was unusual for Yorkshire and Lancashire based senior clubs to risk travelling to Cumbria as the long journey plus playing a tough Cumbrian team on their own pitch were factors that could swing the odds in favour of a possible upset. Losing money on a cup tie by offering to pay generous compensation to switch the game at least reduced the risk of the club becoming victims of a giant killing act. Why Huddersfield took the gamble of playing at Hensingham is not recorded but there is some 'anecdotal' evidence that Huddersfield, who had a number of Cumbrians in their ranks, were persuaded that they could travel to the North West give their Cumbrian players an opportunity to visit their families and also win the game. Huddersfield did win by 33 points to nil, a score that didn't reflect the tough battle in which Hensingham's forwards gave a great display. Over 2,500 spectators watched the tie on what was described in the local newspaper as *'a glorious day'*. Had it rained, the lack of cover at the ground would probably have reduced the attendance to a few hundred. The decision taken by the Hensingham committee to stage the game on their own ground produced the following statement by the local rugby correspondent: '*Their committee has taken a stand which might well serve as an object lesson for other Cumberland clubs in the future and the net result of which is that their supporters are now more enthusiastic than ever.*' The Cumbrians did not become giant killers but they certainly enhanced their reputation. Unfortunately, the impact of the 'object lesson' was not really tested as, for the next few years; very few clubs from Cumbria managed to qualify for the first round proper.

As will be clear from this story so far and will also be confirmed in later chapters, junior clubs tend to have a brief period of success, sometimes just one season, others perhaps two or three seasons. The run of success often ends when some of their leading players move to senior clubs or, on occasions, when the driving force behind the club leaves. Lindley, from Huddersfield, was a club that reached the first round in 1929, 1931 and 1932. In 1929 they lost 32 points to 2 at St Helens and in 1932 they made the long trip to Barrow, losing by 65 points to nil. Their best performance was in 1931 when they played Rochdale Hornets on their home ground on Acre Street, near the centre of the village. In 1929 Lindley had also been drawn at home but had switched the game to St Helens after an offer of £100 compensation. However, in 1931 Rochdale Hornets, because of its difficult financial situation, was unable to offer compensation, and so the junior club prepared to stage the cup tie. On the Saturday morning there was two inches of snow on the pitch and it took twenty to thirty volunteers to clear it so that the game could go ahead. Before the match, the Lindley Brass Band entertained the 2,000 spectators that surrounded

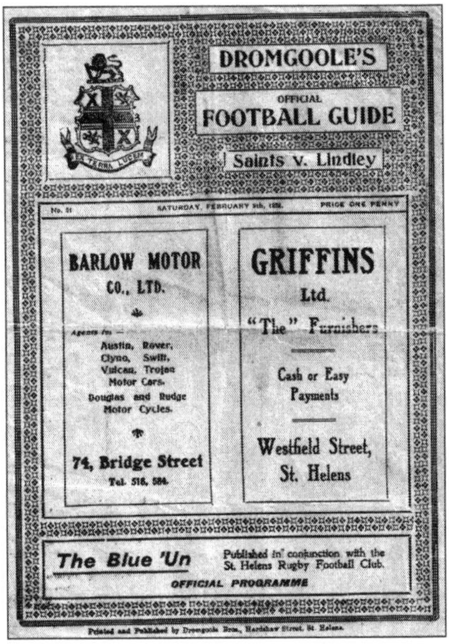

St Helens v Lindley programme 1929

the pitch. The cup tie was a closely contested encounter. The score at half time was 0-0 and Lindley had produced an outstanding display, particularly as they were playing up the slope. In the second half the home supporters were sensing a giant killing act, particularly as mid-way through the second half they only trailed by three points. Unfortunately home hopes were dashed when Clarke, the Lindley scrum half, who had been outstanding, left the field injured. Reduced to twelve men, Lindley conceded two further tries and Rochdale Hornets scraped home by 13 points to 2. It is obviously not possible to say what the result would have been had the tie been played at Rochdale, but a big local support and a tiny village ground with a sloping pitch must have been important factors in the closeness of the score. Rochdale will have breathed a sigh of relief on the final whistle and probably reflected on their journey back to Lancashire that they were lucky to be in the second round.

Lindley 1932

1929 was the year that Uno's Dabs reached the first round of the Cup. This junior club was based in St Helens and its name was associated with a local bookmaker. The story goes that the bookmaker used to run some type of sweep every week with the tickets called tabs or dabs. His real name isn't known but his nickname was Uno. It is not clear whether that is the real reason for the club name, but if it is it could well have been that the bookmaker thought his association with a local rugby team would provide additional publicity for his business. If publicity was what the bookmaker was seeking, he must have benefitted from the press coverage of the three appearances that Uno's Dabs made in the Cup. The 1929 game against Wigan Highfield resulted in what was described in the local newspaper as a rout, with the headline '*Cricket Score at Highfield*'. Highfield registered the highest score in the round, beating Uno's Dabs by 45 points to nil. Uno's Dabs re-appeared in the Cup in 1932 and gave a much better display at Dewsbury. The junior team had been drawn at home but were persuaded by the senior club's officials to switch the game to Crown Flatt and play on a Wednesday afternoon. At half time, with Dewsbury only leading by 11 points to 10, a shock looked possible however, the Crown Flatt men obviously recognised that they needed to improve in the second half and did so to run out 27 points to 10 winners. An attendance of 2,000 was reported with receipts of £140, a figure that disappointed the Dabs officials and also the 44 supporters that made the long journey from St Helens. The junior club had hoped to make at least £150 from switching the tie. Uno's Dabs final Cup appearance came in 1933 when they lost by 42 points to 5 at Halifax. The game had a number of similarities to their previous season's tie at Dewsbury. Tackling ferociously, Uno's Dabs put Halifax under pressure from the first whistle and, although the Dabs struggled to attack against a senior side that monopolised the possession, they never gave up. It was only the loss of Platt, one of their forwards with a head injury that allowed Halifax to take complete control. The seniors extra man advantage resulted in a score that flattered them and did not do justice to the effort put in by the Dabs.

Throughout the 1930s the number of junior clubs involved in the Cup continued to vary. Only two junior clubs took part in the first round in 1936 and 1937, a number that increased in 1938 to three and in 1939 to four. The junior clubs were certainly making up the numbers!

A change in the attitude of senior clubs to their junior counterparts came in 1926 with the proposal, made at the Annual Northern Rugby Football League Conference, to create and support the development of amateur leagues. Concern was expressed at the Conference that unless additional support and encouragement was given to the clubs that were not involved in the Championship then the sport would not continue to thrive. New amateur leagues were set up but some of the leading junior clubs appeared to be reluctant to become involved in these new organisations. Presumably this was because those clubs wished to continue to pay some of their players and play against the second teams of the senior clubs. Featherstone Rovers and Castleford had moved from the junior to the senior ranks by being successful in their own district and putting on a good show in the Cup. It may be, therefore, that there were other clubs with similar aspirations who believed that if they became completely amateur then they were making it much more difficult for themselves to make the step up to the big time. As with many of the changes that have taken place in rugby league since 1895, renaming all the clubs below senior level as amateur was a change that, as mentioned earlier, took many years to be accepted. However, even after the formation of BARLA there is still quite a lot of anecdotal evidence that there were amateur clubs that continued to pay some or all of their players. Therefore, even though amateur rugby league came into existence officially in 1926, for the purposes of this book I will continue to call clubs below senior level 'junior clubs' until 1973.

The junior clubs with unusual names continued with the involvement of the Golden Lions in 1931. Bramley were the opponents for this St Helens club and, according to the match report of their first round game, Bramley were very lucky to scrape home by 7 points to 3. The Golden Lions had a number of opportunities to kick penalties and take an early lead but the heavy ball meant that all the kicks were missed. The second half saw Bramley throw wave after wave of attacks at the Golden Lions line but found it impossible to breech and only sealed the game when the Golden Lions were reduced to eleven men after two of their players were taken from the field injured. In 1931 Keighley also struggled at home against Great Clifton, a Cumbrian village team. The Cumbrians led by 5 points to 3 at half time after taking advantage of the slope to put the Keighley line under tremendous pressure. Keighley managed to snatch the win in the second half with an unconverted try. Prior to the game, Keighley were confident of beating their junior opponents but were concerned about the size of the gate. The attendance of 4,250 was remarkable as torrential rain had turned the pitch into a 'mud bath'. Perhaps with the benefit of hindsight Keighley should have been more concerned about their opponents than the attendance. These games in 1931 are two of only three cup ties in the decade where any junior club came close to beating senior opponents.

The Golden Lions appeared once in the first round proper as did South Yorkshire club Askern Welfare, who in 1933 drew Wigan at home. The story of Askern's involvement in the Challenge Cup is all the more remarkable when you consider that professional rugby league was not played in that part of South Yorkshire until 1951, and that Askern was one of only two junior clubs operating in the district. The other remarkable fact about Askern's involvement is that they staged the cup tie on their own ground. Askern had been formed in 1926 during the coal strike, and in their seven years in existence had won many trophies in the junior game. Initially Wigan were very reluctant to play the game at Askern. It was only a week before it was due to take place, and following a visit by the Wigan secretary, that it was agreed that the tie should be played at the Askern Welfare ground. The result was probably as expected, with Wigan winning by 46 points to nil. However, it must be noted that Askern had to play the second half with twelve men after their captain, Alf Thompson, was carried from the field just before half time with a suspected broken leg. The other factor in the big Wigan score were the eleven goals kicked by Jim Sullivan. He landed them from all parts of the ground. Although the result did not go their way, the decision to stage the game at the Welfare ground was more than justified by the attendance of 4,208, with many of the spectators watching their first ever rugby league match. This cup tie must have made a lasting impression on all the people who witnessed it and was probably one of the biggest sporting events that had ever taken place in the tiny mining village.

Apart from the two results mentioned earlier, the majority of the games in the early 1930s resulted in comfortable victories for the senior outfit, with one or two very one sided games such as Halifax beating Featherstone Juniors 74 points to 9 in 1930 and Barrow beating Maryport 83 points to 3 in 1938. One exception was in 1937 when Goole lost at home by 14 points to 2 to Broughton Rangers. Goole had reached the first round proper by beating Glasson Rangers in Maryport in the final qualifying round. The coach journey to Cumbria took Goole six hours and they only arrived in Maryport, forty five minutes before kick-off. A remarkable attendance of 3,700 watched the game, but because of the chronic unemployment in the town, most of the crowd was allowed in free and the receipts were only £32. The first round game against Broughton Rangers was staged on the Goole home ground, The Victoria Pleasure Grounds. Broughton made a number of offers to Goole to switch the tie but they were refused. An admission price of 1s was agreed with 2/6 being the cost of a seat in the stand. 2,000 people saw a game in which Goole, members of the Castleford and Doncaster League, certainly matched their illustrious senior opponents. With the score at 6 points to nil at half time Goole saw they had a great opportunity to win and after the interval put Broughton under tremendous pressure. The Manchester club just managed to hold out and sealed the game in the last eight minutes with two tries and a conversion.

In 1939, Sharlston Red Rose joined the small group of junior clubs that had managed to stage a Challenge Cup tie on their home ground after the First World War. Drawn at home to Bramley on 4th February, Sharlston overcame the effects of two severe frosts and, with the aid of a quick thaw during the Saturday morning, managed to get their pitch passed fit for play. Many hours of work had been put in by officials, players and supporters on the pitch and on the surrounding area. Their hard work was rewarded with an attendance of 2,500 and gate receipts of £104, but unfortunately not a victory. Sharlston went into the game without two of their best players. Henry Dooler and Sam Speight were both ill, a situation that according to the Wakefield Express match report had seriously affected Sharlston's prospects of reaching the second round. The game began with Sharlston defending heroically and in the first half they kept Bramley in their own twenty five for more than twenty minutes through some ferocious tackling. However, in attack Sharlston struggled to make any inroads and their one try came from an interception. Bramley, on the other hand, gradually wore down their smaller junior opponents, scoring three late tries to seal the victory. The game was magnanimously described in the Wakefield Express as *'one of the outstanding days in the history of the game in the mining village'*.

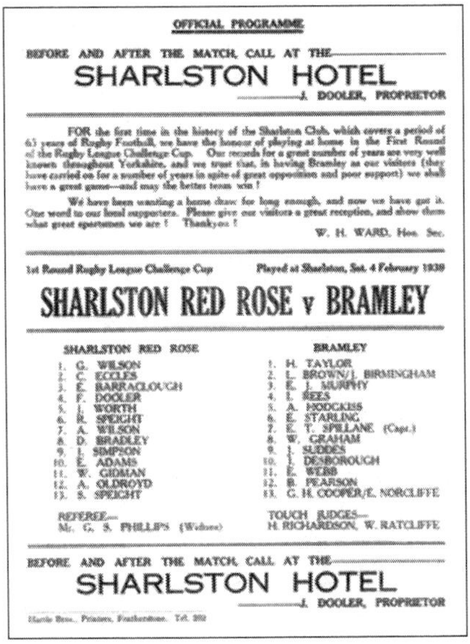

OFFICIAL PROGRAMME

BEFORE AND AFTER THE MATCH, CALL AT THE

SHARLSTON HOTEL

J. DOOLER, PROPRIETOR

FOR the first time in the history of the Sharlston Club, which covers a period of 63 years of Rugby Football, we have the honour of playing at home in the First Round of the Rugby League Challenge Cup. Our records for a great number of years are very well known throughout Yorkshire, and we trust that, in having Bramley as our visitors (they have carried on for a number of years in spite of great opposition and poor support) we shall have a great game—and may the better team win!

We have been wanting a home draw for long enough, and now we have got it. One word to our local supporters. Please give our visitors a great reception, and show them what great sportsmen we are! Thankyou!

W. H. WARD, Hon. Sec.

1st Round Rugby League Challenge Cup — Played at Sharlston, Sat. 4 February 1939

SHARLSTON RED ROSE v BRAMLEY

SHARLSTON RED ROSE	BRAMLEY
1. G. WILSON	1. H. TAYLOR
2. C. ECCLES	2. L. BROWN/J. BIRMINGHAM
3. E. BARRACLOUGH	3. E. J. MURPHY
4. F. DOOLER	4. I. REES
5. J. WORTH	5. A. HODGKISS
6. R. SPEIGHT	6. E. STARLING
7. A. WILSON	7. E. T. SPILLANE (Capt.)
8. D. BRADLEY	8. W. GRAHAM
9. J. SIMPSON	9. J. SUDDES
10. E. ADAMS	10. J. DESBOROUGH
11. W. GIDMAN	11. E. WEBB
12. A. OLDROYD	12. B. PEARSON
13. S. SPEIGHT	13. G. H. COOPER/E. NORCLIFFE

REFEREE— Mr. G. S. PHILLIPS (Widnes)

TOUCH JUDGES— H. RICHARDSON, W. RATCLIFFE

BEFORE AND AFTER THE MATCH, CALL AT THE

SHARLSTON HOTEL

J. DOOLER, PROPRIETOR

Sharlston v Bramley team sheet 1939

The cup draws in the 1920s and 1930s were not kind to the juniors, with many of them facing leading clubs from the Championship and very few of them having the advantage of being drawn at home. However, despite the vagaries of the draw there were some exciting encounters, and the games staged by Askern and Sharlston, were events that will have lived long in the memories of both the players and spectators.

The 1939 competition was the last one played before the onset of World War Two. It was to be the 1945/46 season before clubs were again able to compete for the Challenge Cup and the prize of a trip to Wembley for the eventual finalists.

Chapter 5

Two Legs

The first Cup competition after World War Two was held in the 1945/46 season. During the War, emergency league and cup competitions had taken place for the senior clubs still able to operate but no junior clubs had taken part in the Cup. Junior rugby league did continue to be played but it was often localised, with travel restrictions making it very difficult for the clubs still operating to play outside their district. Also, in strong rugby league areas, many of the men who might have continued to play rugby had either been called up into the Forces or were working long hours in reserved occupations. The junior clubs that did continue to play would, therefore, field teams made up of young men who hadn't been called up and servicemen home on leave, plus a few stalwarts who, under normal circumstances, would have retired from the game. Rugby Union did continue to be played during the War, with most big towns and cities having at least one club still operating. Most of those clubs were very happy to welcome rugby league players, whether professional or amateur. As junior clubs did not have the opportunity to play senior opposition during the War, there may have been an increased expectation that the resumption of normal activities in 1945 would lead to a widening of the gap in playing standards and an increase in the size of winning margins for the senior clubs. However, the reality was very different.

There were just twenty seven clubs taking part in the Championship in the 1945/46 season. The nine clubs that returned to action after closing down during the hostilities, plus Workington Town who joined the senior ranks in 1945, were added to the seventeen that had managed to continue to play during wartime. With only twenty seven clubs, the RFL decided that the first round of the Challenge Cup would be played over two legs. This was a way of increasing revenue as all the senior clubs, irrespective of the draw, would have a home game in the first round. It was probably surprising just how close many of the first round games were, particularly in the late 1940s. During the War, many of the professional clubs had managed to continue operating, often by using players from other clubs that were in the Forces and stationed in their area. Clubs like Dewsbury actively recruited many of the leading players and as a result became much stronger than they had been pre-war. Once the War ended and players returned to their own clubs, some of the successful wartime outfits had to build up their playing strength again. This was a difficult task when many of the professional players still in the Forces were not immediately demobilised. The re-building that the senior clubs had to undertake in the late 1940s presented an opportunity to some of the junior clubs, particularly those that had re-organised quickly, to really challenge and, in some cases, beat their senior opponents in the new two legged first round.

There were five junior clubs involved in the first round in 1946. Three rounds of qualifying had taken place, not as many as had usually been played pre-war, but enough to suggest that the junior game was beginning to recover. Higher Ince were drawn against Widnes and struggled to compete in both legs, as did Hull Juniors who played Bramley, but with the other three junior clubs it was a different story. Langworthy Juniors played their first leg game at Hull Kingston Rovers and lost by 18 points to nil on a very heavy pitch and with a greasy ball that made handling difficult. Langworthy had opportunities to score, but according to the Hull Daily Mail report, *'either lacked finishing speed or made tactical errors'*. The Salford based club was praised for its efforts in defence but Hull Kingston Rovers were confident going into the second leg, which was much closer with Rovers scraping home by 14 points to 7. But the reality was that the senior club was never in any real danger of being beaten. Kells came very close to beating Warrington in their first leg at home only losing by 3 points to nil. Warrington had travelled

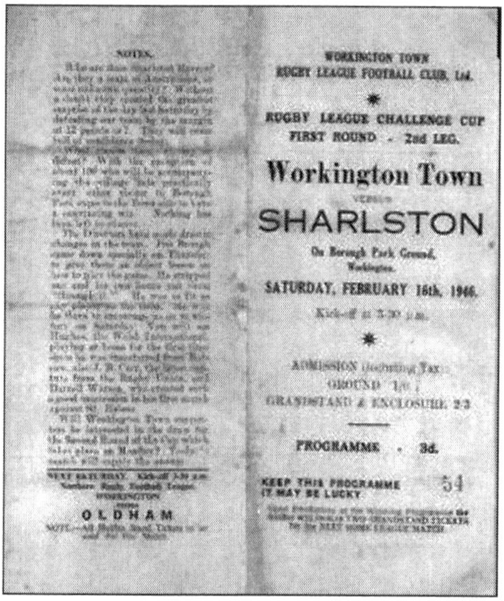

Workington v Sharlston programme 1946

to Cumbria expecting an easy win but a combination of a heavy pitch and enthusiastic tackling by Kells restricted the Warrington score to one unconverted try. In the second leg at Warrington's Wilderspool ground on a much better pitch, the senior club were soon in control. In the second half they took advantage of some ill-discipline from Kells robust forwards to record a much more convincing win. They moved into the second round by winning the tie by 27 points to nil. The consolation for Kells was a share of the £1,000 gate receipts from the two games. However, in 1946 pride of place must go to Sharlston Rovers who became the first club since 1909 to defeat senior opposition in the Challenge Cup. Unfortunately they did not progress to the second round, as their opponents Workington Town managed to win the second leg and score enough points to overturn Sharlston's first leg advantage. As had been the case in 1939, Sharlston were determined to stage the home leg on their own ground. A band of willing volunteers worked hard to erect fencing and canvas screens around the pitch in anticipation of an attendance of 3,000. Unfortunately, the attendance did not match expectations but was still an impressive 1,200. But, what was even more impressive was the Sharlston performance which saw them win the first leg by 12 points to 7. The Sharlston team was captained by Tommy Fox, the father of the famous Fox brothers Neil, Don and Peter. Tommy Fox had come out of retirement, and at the age of thirty nine gave a performance that belied his years. Workington Town, new to the senior ranks, had nevertheless made a good start in the league and were not really expected to struggle against a tiny village club. But the Workington Star's match report recognised just how well Sharlston played, reporting that the '*tenacity and grit of the young Sharlston forwards, who's marking and tackling upset the visitors play*'. The Sharlston victory was well deserved and after the game one hundred and fifty players, officials and supporters sat down to a celebration meal in the Working Men's Club. The meal was prepared by the women of the village who, despite rationing, had managed to make and collect enough food to provide an impressive spread. Sharlston travelled to the second leg full of confidence and over 9,000 spectators were at Workington's Borough Park ground so see whether the juniors could provide another upset. With a half time score of just 2 points to nil to Workington, the tie was in the balance as Sharlston still led on aggregate. In the end, however, Workington's greater experience proved too much for the gallant juniors and the Cumbrians sealed the game in the last fifteen minutes to give an aggregate score of 23 points to 14 and a passage into the second round.

The 1947 Cup competition was greatly affected by the terrible winter weather, with many of the first round ties delayed until early March. Workington Town featured again in one of the junior versus senior clashes when they were drawn against Widnes Dragons. The Dragons had operated prior to World War Two, and it was a group of players that had played in the 1930s that were instrumental in re-starting the club after the War. The Dragons decided to travel to Cumbria for the first leg by coach and a combination of poor weather and hold ups meant that they arrived in Workington an hour late. A number of the players had to get changed on the coach and it was perhaps the chaotic start to the tie that contributed to their heavy defeat. Workington scored 48 points without reply and the expectation was that the second leg would see a similarly big score and a comfortable passage into the second round for the Cumbrians. The second leg was held at Naughton Park, the Widnes senior club's home ground, and although the winning margin wasn't as great as in the first leg, Workington were always in control, winning by 21 points to 5 and the round on aggregate by 69 points to 5.There were 9,035 spectators at the first leg at Borough Park and 3,080 at the second leg, so both clubs will have benefitted financially. The other three ties in 1947 all resulted in comfortable aggregate victories for the seniors. Warrington had two easy wins when they played Brookland Rovers with both games taking place at Warrington. The legendary Australian winger Brian Bevan, a prolific Warrington try scorer, proved too much of a handful for the juniors and contributed three tries in the first leg. Despite the one sided score lines, Brookland Rovers did compete enthusiastically in both games. Over 21,000 spectators saw the two ties contributing an impressive £1,735 in gate receipts. The other two ties between Pemberton Rovers and Liverpool Stanley and Halifax and Wheldale Colliery were very competitive with the scores indicating close games both home and away. Due to the terrible winter, Liverpool Stanley had to use the Warrington ground for their home leg against Pemberton Rovers, and the 4,000 attendance could well have been larger than if the game had been played in Liverpool. Halifax's home leg against Wheldale Colliery was also played at a neutral venue. Hunslet hosted the tie on a Wednesday afternoon, presumably because

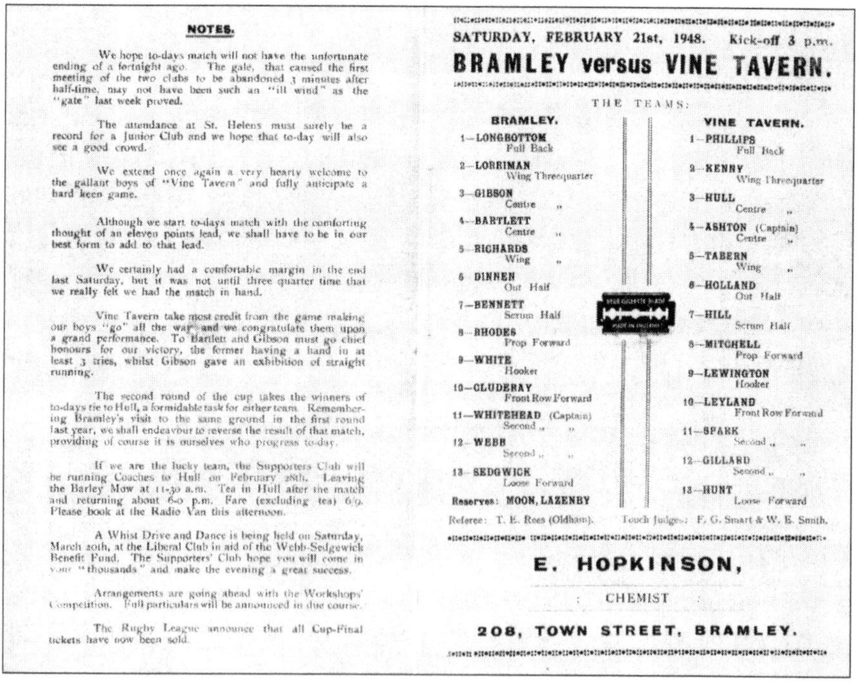

NOTES.

We hope to-days match will not have the unfortunate ending of a fortnight ago. The gale, that caused the first meeting of the two clubs to be abandoned 3 minutes after half-time, may not have been such an "ill wind" as the "gate" last week proved.

The attendance at St. Helens must surely be a record for a Junior Club and we hope that to-day will also see a good crowd.

We extend once again a very hearty welcome to the gallant boys of "Vine Tavern" and fully anticipate a hard keen game.

Although we start to-days match with the comforting thought of an eleven points lead, we shall have to be in our best form to add to that lead.

We certainly had a comfortable margin in the end last Saturday, but it was not until three quarter time that we really felt we had the match in hand.

Vine Tavern take most credit from the game making our boys "go" all the way and we congratulate them upon a grand performance. To Bartlett and Gibson must go chief honours for our victory, the former having a hand in at least 3 tries, whilst Gibson gave an exhibition of straight running.

The second round of the cup takes the winners of to-days tie to Hull, a formidable task for either team. Remembering Bramley's visit to the same ground in the first round last year, we shall endeavour to reverse the result of that match, providing of course it is ourselves who progress to-day.

If we are the lucky team, the Supporters Club will be running Coaches to Hull on February 28th. Leaving the Barley Mow at 11-30 a.m. Tea in Hull after the match and returning about 6-0 p.m. Fare (excluding tea) 6/0. Please book at the Radio Van this afternoon.

A Whist Drive and Dance is being held on Saturday, March 20th, at the Liberal Club in aid of the Webb-Sedgewick Benefit Fund. The Supporters' Club hope you will come in your "thousands" and make the evening a great success.

Arrangements are going ahead with the Workshops' Competition. Full particulars will be announced in due course.

The Rugby League announce that all Cup-Final tickets have now been sold.

SATURDAY, FEBRUARY 21st, 1948. Kick-off 3 p.m.

BRAMLEY versus VINE TAVERN.

THE TEAMS:

BRAMLEY.	VINE TAVERN.
1—LONGBOTTOM Full Back	1—PHILLIPS Full Back
2—LORRIMAN Wing Threequarter	2—KENNY Wing Threequarter
3—GIBSON Centre ,,	3—HULL Centre ,,
4—BARTLETT Centre ,,	4—ASHTON (Captain) Centre ,,
5—RICHARDS Wing ,,	5—TABERN Wing ,,
6—DINNEN Out Half	6—HOLLAND Out Half
7—BENNETT Scrum Half	7—HILL Scrum Half
8—RHODES Prop Forward	8—MITCHELL Prop Forward
9—WHITE Hooker	9—LEWINGTON Hooker
10—CLUDERAY Front Row Forward	10—LEYLAND Front Row Forward
11—WHITEHEAD (Captain) Second ,, ,,	11—SPARK Second ,, ,,
12—WEBB Second ,, ,,	12—GILLARD Second ,, ,,
13—SEDGWICK Loose Forward	13—HUNT Loose Forward
Reserves: MOON, LAZENBY	

Referee: T. E. Rees (Oldham). Touch Judges: F. G. Smart & W. E. Smith.

E. HOPKINSON,

CHEMIST

208, TOWN STREET, BRAMLEY.

Bramley v Vine Tavern programme 1948

the Halifax ground was unfit. Only four juniors made up the numbers in 1947 as Leigh had re-formed, taking the Championship to twenty eight clubs.

Four clubs also took part in 1948 with two remarkable ties standing out. Bramley hosted Vine Tavern, from St Helens, in the first leg with the game being abandoned after forty three minutes when gale force winds blew one of the goal posts down. Fortunately, nobody was injured but with the score standing at 3 – 3 the game had to be replayed. The second leg was played at Knowlsley Road, the St Helens ground, before the two clubs had been able to re-play the abandoned first leg. Despite Bramley probably being one of least attractive of the senior clubs, a remarkable attendance of 14,000 was recorded. At half-time, Vine

Established 1880 Personal Supervision at all times

W. G. DIXON LTD.

Complete Funeral and Private Hire Service

Rolls Royce Limousines and Wedding Cars

4 BICKERSTAFFE STREET, ST. HELENS

Tel. 2007 (Office) Tel. 2860 (Residence)

The Vine Tavern team came into existence in the season 1945-6 largely through the initiative of Alf. Bowen, once a member of the City Road team. They did well in the Junior League Medal Competition, losing to Ring-o'-Bells in the semi-final.

The next season saw them settling down to real football and they won the St. Helens and District Junior League Competition, losing only three games in the season.

This year the Committee has had the assistance of Frank Bowen, brilliant on his day both as a forward and a back, with the Recs of twenty years ago, and now as landlord of the Vine Tavern is a kind of godfather to the team. Another clever footballer who has helped this year to get the " Vine " where they are, is Arthur Cross, their trainer. A good judge of a player and understanding in his handling of men the " Vine " committee have done well in choosing him.

They have not lost a game this season and in their 17 matches they have scored 353 points against their opponents 51. Including last week's match at Bramley they have scored 60 points in the Challenge Cup Competition against 10.

Telephone 2846

MOTOR REPAIRS

by Skilled Engineers

at the

FINGERPOST GARAGE

MARSH STREET

ST. HELENS

Saturday, February 14th, 1948 Price 2d.

TO-DAY'S TEAMS

Vine Tavern		Bramley	
Full Back:		Full Back:	
1	J. PHILLIPS	1	LONGBOTTOM
Threequarters:		Threequarters:	
2	J. KENNY	2	RICHARDS
3	W. HARRISON	3	GIBSON
4	B. ASHTON, (Capt.)	4	BARTLETT
5	J. HULL	5	LORRIMAN
Half Backs:		Half Backs:	
6	R. TABERN	6	DINNEN
7	W. HILL	7	BENNETT
Forwards:		Forwards:	
8	JOHN MITCHELL	8	RHODES
9	J. LEWINGTON	9	WHITE
10	T. LEYLAND	10	HARRISON
11	T. SPARK	11	WEBB
12	F. GILLARD	12	CRAVEN
13	J. HUNT	13	WHITEHEAD

SWIFTS

Referee: T. ARMITAGE

Linesmen: J. HEATON, (Red) J. G. EVANS, (Blue)

For Modern Equipment and Book-keeping Methods

GET IN TOUCH with CECIL DROMGOOLE

THE MODERN PRESS

BICKERSTAFFE STREET

ST. HELENS

Telephone 2013

Vine Tavern v Bramley programme 1948

Tavern were in contention with the scores level at 3-3. However, the second half belonged to Bramley and they managed to win by 17 points to 6. Vine Tavern took a great deal of confidence from their display and went back to Bramley for the first leg replay with high hopes. The game at Bramley's Barley Mow ground was played on a snow covered pitch and Bramley just had the edge, winning by 10 points to 2.

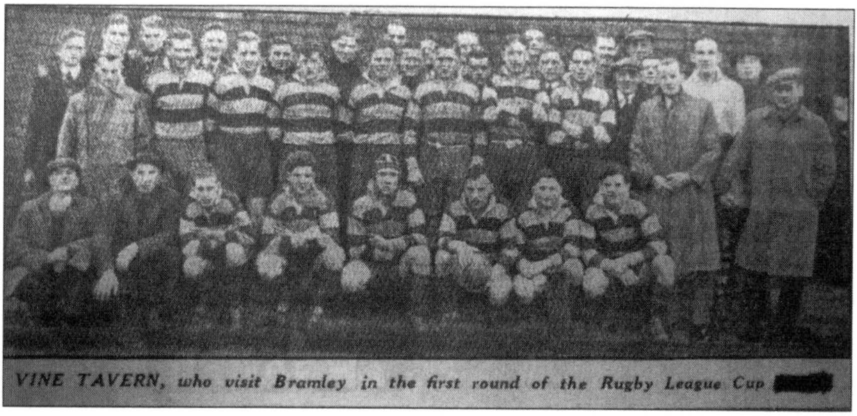

Vine Tavern 1948

The giant killing act in 1948 took place in Cumbria when Risehow and Gillhead played Keighley at Derwent Park in Workington. The Colliery team, from Maryport, had given Keighley a shock in the first leg with a courageous display, in the mud, restricting their senior opponents to just eleven points. Therefore the second leg in Cumbria provided a real opportunity for Risehow and Gillhead to progress to the next round. The game had an 11.00am kick to avoid clashing with Workington Town's home tie against Warrington just down the road at Borough Park. At Derwent Park over 5,000 supporters saw Risehow and Gillhead put up a tremendous performance and with ten minutes left looked to have sealed a remarkable victory. Ike Fearon charged down a Keighley kick but was unable to catch the ball for what would have been a certain try and the opportunity for a conversion to win the round on aggregate. As it was although they won the game by 10 points to 2 Risehow and Gillhead went out of the Cup despite having achieved a famous victory over senior opposition. An interesting footnote to the Keighley versus Risehow and Gillhead ties was the fact that as the attendance for the first leg was only 2,000, and Keighley made a loss on the game. Their share of the gate, after expenses, amounting to just £61, insufficient to play the winning money the players earned winning the first leg. How the Keighley club dealt with the financial loss from the first leg may have affected the players' attitude in the second leg. If there was no winning money available for the game in Cumbria, could that help to explain the defeat? We may never know. Rochdale Hornets had two tough games against Pemberton Rovers. In the first leg, at Rochdale, 3,000 spectators saw the teams deadlocked 0-0 at half time. Rochdale managed to score thirteen points in the second half to take a lead into the second leg. The juniors must have been confident of overturning the lead when the second leg was played at Wigan's ground. The game attracted 8,677 spectators to Central Park, but despite another valiant effort from Pemberton they were not able cross the Rochdale line and lost the tie by 11 points to nil. The final junior involvement in 1948 saw St Helens play Buslingthorpe Vale, from Leeds. The first leg at St Helens was very one sided with the senior club winning easily by 48 points to nil. However, in the second leg, played at Headingley in front of 3,180 spectators, Buslingthorpe Vale put on a very different performance, matching their senior opponents through a combination of tough tackling and in the opinion of the reporter from St Helens a disregard for the offside rules. In his match report for the St Helens Reporter he stated that *'Offside at the scrum was the rule not the exception. Their centres stood or ran offside at every scrum. Very effective it was!* Buslingthorpe Vale took an early lead with a penalty and with the score at 5 points to 2 at half time a shock was a possibility. The Leeds club were never going to win on aggregate but a victory over senior opposition did seem to within their grasp. However, it wasn't to be, and in the second half St Helens scored two more tries to seal their victory by 13 points to 2.

As the number of senior clubs playing in the Championship continued to fluctuate, from one season to the next, so the number of junior clubs making up the numbers varied. In 1949 there were three junior clubs involved in the first round proper. One of them was Normanton, a previous giant killer who came close to providing an upset again when they met Belle Vue Rangers at Wakefield Trinity's ground. The decision to play the first leg at the professional club's ground had been widely criticised locally. However, an attendance of 6,500 more than justified Normanton's decision, particularly as the second leg at the Belle Vue Rangers ground produced an attendance of only 3,000. Normanton put up a very good performance in the first leg and Belle Vue Rangers had to rely on dropped goals in order to take a lead into the second leg. For their trip to Manchester Normanton took over 400 of their own supporters. The second leg was also very close with Belle Vue Rangers just having the edge. The aggregate score of 21 points 4 did not really

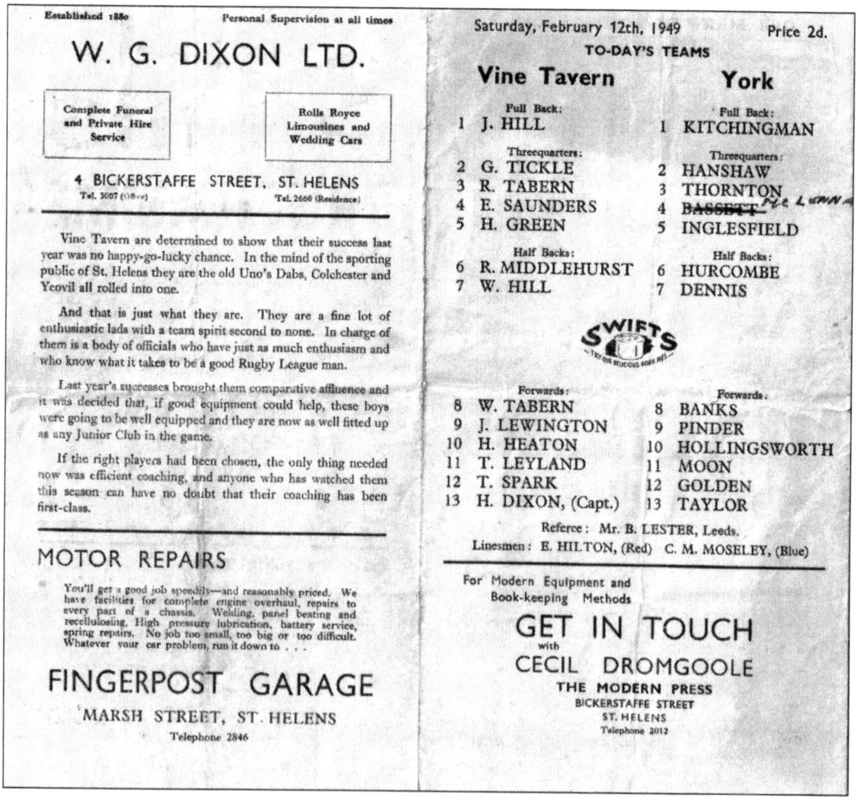
Established 1880 — Personal Supervision at all times

W. G. DIXON LTD.

Complete Funeral and Private Hire Service

Rolls Royce Limousines and Wedding Cars

4 BICKERSTAFFE STREET, ST. HELENS

Tel. 3007 (Office) — Tel. 2660 (Residence)

Vine Tavern are determined to show that their success last year was no happy-go-lucky chance. In the mind of the sporting public of St. Helens they are the old Uno's Dabs, Colchester and Yeovil all rolled into one.

And that is just what they are. They are a fine lot of enthusiastic lads with a team spirit second to none. In charge of them is a body of officials who have just as much enthusiasm and who know what it takes to be a good Rugby League man.

Last year's successes brought them comparative affluence and it was decided that, if good equipment could help, these boys were going to be well equipped and they are now as well fitted up as any Junior Club in the game.

If the right players had been chosen, the only thing needed now was efficient coaching, and anyone who has watched them this season can have no doubt that their coaching has been first-class.

MOTOR REPAIRS

You'll get a good job speedily—and reasonably priced. We have facilities for complete engine overhaul, repairs to every part of a chassis. Welding, panel beating and recellulosing. High pressure lubrication, battery service, spring repairs. No job too small, too big or too difficult. Whatever your car problem, run it down to . . .

FINGERPOST GARAGE

MARSH STREET, ST. HELENS

Telephone 2846

Saturday, February 12th, 1949 — Price 2d.

TO-DAY'S TEAMS

Vine Tavern		York	
Full Back:		Full Back:	
1	J. HILL	1	KITCHINGMAN
Threequarters:		Threequarters:	
2	G. TICKLE	2	HANSHAW
3	R. TABERN	3	THORNTON
4	E. SAUNDERS	4	~~BASSETT~~
5	H. GREEN	5	INGLESFIELD
Half Backs:		Half Backs:	
6	R. MIDDLEHURST	6	HURCOMBE
7	W. HILL	7	DENNIS
Forwards:		Forwards:	
8	W. TABERN	8	BANKS
9	J. LEWINGTON	9	PINDER
10	H. HEATON	10	HOLLINGSWORTH
11	T. LEYLAND	11	MOON
12	T. SPARK	12	GOLDEN
13	H. DIXON, (Capt.)	13	TAYLOR

SWIFTS

Referee: Mr. B. LESTER, Leeds.

Linesmen: E. HILTON, (Red) C. M. MOSELEY, (Blue)

For Modern Equipment and Book-keeping Methods

GET IN TOUCH with CECIL DROMGOOLE

THE MODERN PRESS

BICKERSTAFFE STREET

ST. HELENS

Telephone 2012

Vine Tavern v York programme 1949

reflect the struggle that Belle Vue Rangers had in overcoming their junior opponents. Vine Tavern, although not giant killers had come very close the previous year to beating Bramley and no doubt York, their opponents in 1949, would have been well aware of the potential for an upset. The first leg was played at the St Helens ground and 6,401 spectators saw Vine Tavern match York in all aspects of the game. With no score from either side at half time an upset did seem possible, at the end of the game just seven points separated the teams with York winning by 11 points to 4. Vine Tavern were very confident going into the second leg and, with six coach loads of supporters to cheer them on, went to York expecting to win. Unfortunately, the juniors struggled to contain their enthusiasm, which resulted in them conceding numerous penalties for 'overzealous' play. York punished their indiscretions to win the tie by 17 points to nil. The consolation for Vine Tavern was a share of the overall receipts of £795. Cumbrian club Broughton Moor also appeared again the Challenge Cup, only to make an unceremonious exit conceding 65 points over the two legs against Oldham.

Broughton Moor was one of the three junior clubs that appeared in the 1950 competition and they fared no better than they had in 1949. In the two legs against Wakefield Trinity they conceded 101 points. Worsley Boys Club, the other junior representative, did a little better against Hunslet, only conceding 63 points. However, as forty five of those were scored in the first leg, played at Wigan's ground, the second leg at Hunslet was unlikely to see Worsley progressing to round two. The 18 points to 9 win by Hunslet in the second leg was described in the Yorkshire Post report as a '*practice match*'. The disappointing attendance of 3,300 probably reflected the view amongst the Hunslet supporters, that the game was a 'dead rubber'. Cardiff, a club that two years later joined the senior ranks, played Salford in the first leg at Abertillery and in a very close game lost by just 15 points to 10. Cardiff led 8 points to 7 at half time but could not press home their advantage in the second half. Ironically it was a Welshman, Jack Davies, playing at stand-off for Salford who was described in the match report as the leading figure in the victory for the senior club. The second leg, at Salford, wasn't

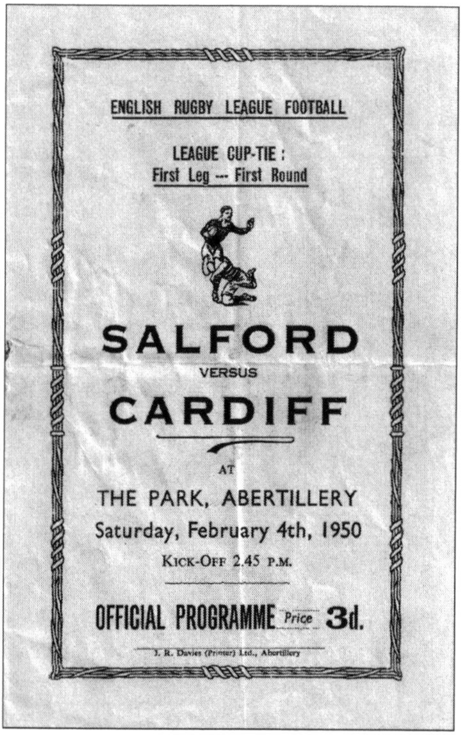
ENGLISH RUGBY LEAGUE FOOTBALL

LEAGUE CUP-TIE :
First Leg — First Round

SALFORD
VERSUS
CARDIFF

AT
THE PARK, ABERTILLERY
Saturday, February 4th, 1950
KICK-OFF 2.45 P.M.

OFFICIAL PROGRAMME Price 3d.

J. R. Davies (Printer) Ltd., Abertillery

Cardiff v Salford programme 1950

quite as close. Cardiff's display was described as plucky but Salford had too much skill and although it wasn't until the second half that they pressed home their advantage Salford were in the end comfortable 20 points to 5 winners.

Broughton Moor took part in the first round again in 1951 with similar heavy defeats as in the previous two years. This time it was Batley they faced and 77 points to 3 was the aggregate score. As Latchford Albion, the other junior club, conceded 62 points, perhaps there were some senior clubs that began to question why, when the first leg of the first round produced such a one sided result, was there was any need to play a second leg. Broughton Moor, Worsley Boys Club and Latchford Albion had all been heavily beaten in their first leg games, rendering the second leg virtually meaningless – a factor that should have affected the attendance for those second leg games. Surprisingly, in the second leg between Latchford and Leigh, played at Warrington's ground, this was not the case. Over 6,500 spectators saw Latchford put up a very disciplined performance on a pitch described as a 'mud bath'. The juniors did not concede a penalty during the whole of the eighty minutes, in stark contrast to Leigh who were continually penalised for off side. A very weary Leigh team trooped off the pitch at the end, relieved to hear the final whistle. Leigh had scored sufficient points in the first leg to guarantee a place in the next round, and would probably have felt a tough second leg played on a heavy pitch was unnecessary. However, the excellent gate at Warrington must have been some consolation. The other club that took part in the Challenge Cup in 1951 was Llanelli. A Welsh League comprising eight clubs had been playing in a semi-professional competition that had been in existence since 1949. Llanelli, like Cardiff in 1950, had won the Welsh League the previous season and were regarded as one of the strongest Welsh clubs at the time. There was a Welsh qualifying section for the Challenge Cup and in the final Llanelli beat Ysytradgynlais by 14 points to 8 to qualify for a place in the first round. Unfortunately, the draw wasn't kind to the Welshmen. They were drawn against Barrow, a club that although in the lower half of the Championship had an impressive reputation in knockout games and in fact reached the Cup Final in 1951. In the first leg at Penygaer Field, in Llanelli, just 1,311 spectators saw the Welshmen put in a good performance. The Welsh Champions led for sixty minutes but the Western Mail reported that a combination of '*greater stamina and better training*' gave Barrow the edge in the last twenty minutes. With a 23 points to 9 victory, the Cumbrian club had established a lead that was unlikely to be overtaken in the second leg. Barrow had made a significant financial loss on the first leg. The gate receipts of £70, after entertainment tax had been deducted, meant that Barrow's share was about £20 hardly sufficient to cover the £100 travel and accommodation costs, winning pay of £8 a player and compensation to the players for loss of work on the Friday before the game. The Barrow club were hoping for a good attendance in the second leg in order to help them to recoup some of their losses. There were 6,530 spectators at the second leg game, a pleasant surprise, as Barrow were expected to win easily. The Cumbrians didn't play particularly well but still managed a 39 points to 5 victory. Llanelli tackled hard but could not handle the pace of the Barrow backs, well marshalled by the legendary Willie Horne. By the early 1950s, the poor attendances for the second legs of many of the first round games must have encouraged the senior clubs to begin discussions about reverting to a straight knockout in the first round.

In 1952, a discussion was held at a Rugby League Council meeting regarding the value of the two leg first round and clubs were asked for their views, however, no decision was reached. There were thirty one clubs playing in the Championship in 1952 and so only Rylands Recreation, from the junior game took part in the Cup. Rylands had had a tough route to the first round. Their final qualifying game involved a long journey to South Wales where they beat Bridgend. In the first round they were drawn against Whitehaven and had to travel to the North West for the first leg. In front of 7,004 spectators, Whitehaven managed a controversial 16 points to nil win. The controversy was caused by the white ball that was used in the game. Rylands said it was much too light and made handling very difficult but their Cumbrian opponents coped with it to take a reasonable lead into the second leg. When the second leg was played at Warrington's ground, 7,814 spectators saw Rylands put up a tremendous performance that for three quarters of the game looked sufficient to produce a victory. However, in the end it was not to be and the 9 -9 draw meant that Whitehaven's winning margin in the first leg was enough for them to progress to the next round.

The 1953 and 1954 Cup competitions did nothing to convince the senior clubs that it was worth continuing with a two leg first round. In 1953 Orford Tannery and NDLB, from Hull, both suffered heavy first leg defeats. In 1954 it was a similar situation with Latchford Albion and Wheldale Colliery both losing heavily in their first leg games, so therefore change was inevitable.

In March 1954, by a show of hands at a Rugby League Council meeting, the senior clubs decided to return to a straight knockout in the Challenge Cup first round. The decision was confirmed at an Emergency General Meeting of the clubs in May 1954. The two leg first round had certainly produced some interesting ties and some very good attendances, particularly in the immediate post War period, but in the eyes of the senior clubs it had outlived its usefulness. For the junior clubs, the late 1940s did not see any of them progress to the second round but it did produce some memorable games, two senior club scalps and a considerable amount of income flowing into junior club coffers. The Second World War had certainly had an impact on playing standards and perhaps, for a few years, the gap between junior and senior clubs did narrow. However, by 1954 and the change back to a straight knockout in the first round, the gap in standards was probably as wide as it had been at any time in the history of the Cup.

Chapter 6

The Barren Years

Over the forty years after the decision in 1954 to end the practice of playing the first round over two legs, the contribution of the junior clubs to the Cup appeared to be just ensuring that there were always thirty two balls in the bag for the first round draw. The involvement of junior clubs over the previous fifty eight years of the competition had been very inconsistent. When all the clubs, whether senior or junior, were allowed to enter, it did give the impression that the Cup was a competition for the whole game. This view had certainly changed over time so that by the 1950s the qualifying rounds seemed to be regarded as a competition for junior clubs where the prize was a place in the first round proper. The problem with that was the number of winners of the qualifying competition varied from year to year depending upon how many clubs were needed to make up the numbers in the first round proper. The constantly changing number of clubs that qualified did not seem to deter junior clubs from entering the qualifying rounds. There were over one hundred junior clubs taking part in the qualifying rounds most seasons. In some years up to eight qualifying rounds were required to find the junior clubs that would take part in the first round proper. However, despite the large number of clubs that did take part in the qualifying rounds, the lack of publicity given to the competition prior to the first round proper probably confirmed the view, within the sport that the Challenge Cup was a competition for the senior clubs. The contribution made to the folklore and history of the Cup by Normanton, Beverley, Sharlston Rovers and Risehow and Gillhead seemed to have either been forgotten or perhaps was considered unimportant. Some of the impressive attendances generated, particularly in the late 1940s when junior clubs played senior clubs, also seemed to have been forgotten. The junior game was in decline by the mid-1950s and 'lip service' was being paid to the need to support and develop the clubs at a junior level. As we move into the 1960s and the beginning of the 1970s, this lack of support and interest in the sport below senior level ultimately led to the formation of the British Amateur Rugby League Association. This chapter deals with the period from 1955 until 1973. I imagine this was a time when a senior club drawing a junior club in the first round saw the draw as one that would probably not produce a good attendance but should certainly guarantee a place in the next round.

Blackpool Borough joined the senior ranks in 1954 and, as there were now thirty one clubs in the Championship in 1955, only one junior club was involved in the first round proper. Dewsbury Celtic was the club that made up the numbers, but a 43 points to nil defeat at Workington Town set a trend of big defeats for junior clubs that continued right up to 1962. The Championship was reduced to thirty clubs at the end of the 1954/55 season when Belle Vue Rangers folded and so for the next few years two junior clubs were allowed into the Cup. The one sided games continued and at least one of the senior clubs drawing a junior club recorded a score of over fifty points every season, irrespective of who the opposition was. The other senior versus junior clash in the first round, if it did not produce a fifty point winning margin, usually produced a winning

Rugby League Challenge Cup
FIRST ROUND

BROOKHOUSE
V
DONCASTER

at

BARNSLEY ROAD PLAYING FIELDS
WAKEFIELD

SATURDAY, 10th FEBRUARY
1962

Kick-off 3-0 p.m.

ADMISSION 2/-

Printed and Published by J. L. Walker, 6 Lawefield Lane, Wakefield. Tel. 2384

Brookhouse v Doncaster programme 1962

score of over thirty points, so indicating another very one-sided game. This depressing sequence continued until Brookhouse drew Doncaster in 1962. Doncaster were near the bottom of the Championship and, as Brookhouse were regarded as one of the best junior clubs, perhaps it would be the year that the run of depressing one- sided junior versus senior clashes came to an end. Brookhouse, formally known as Wakefield Loco, played their home games on Barnsley Road Recreation Ground in Wakefield. They decided to retain home advantage and stage the game on their own ground after Doncaster insisted that it must be played on the Saturday afternoon, despite Wakefield Trinity also being at home on the same day. Staging a Challenge Cup game on a park pitch is a hard enough task without the fact that a few hundred yards away Wakefield Trinity were entertaining Warrington in a cup tie that attracted 19,330 spectators. However, the Brookhouse club was not daunted by their task both off and on the field. Over 600 spectators crowded round the pitch to watch the juniors put in an outstanding performance that saw them leading by 4 points to 2 with two minutes to go. Sadly the giant killing act was not to be, as in the 78th minute Peter Goodchild, the Doncaster winger, crashed over in the corner to score a try that was converted from the touchline by Doncaster's loose forward Ron Swales, after which the referee blew the whistle for full-time. The Brookhouse result began a trend of much closer senior versus junior clashes in the 1960s.

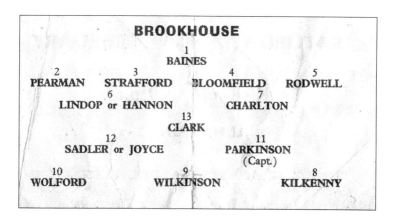

BROOKHOUSE

1 BAINES

2 PEARMAN | 3 STRAFFORD | 4 BLOOMFIELD | 5 RODWELL

6 LINDOP or HANNON | 7 CHARLTON

13 CLARK

12 SADLER or JOYCE | 11 PARKINSON (Capt.)

10 WOLFORD | 9 WILKINSON | 8 KILKENNY

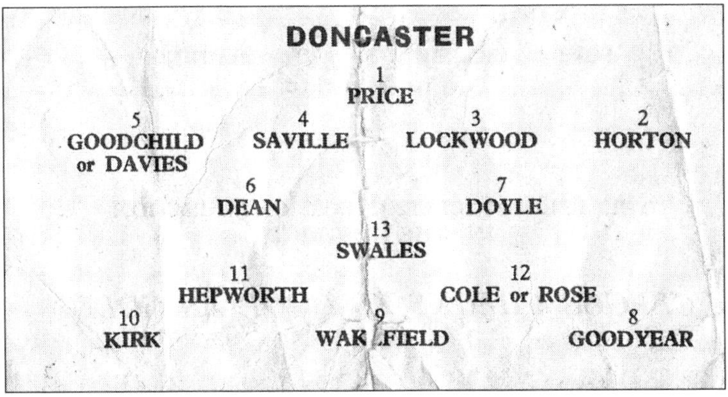

DONCASTER

1 PRICE

5 GOODCHILD or DAVIES — 4 SAVILLE — 3 LOCKWOOD — 2 HORTON

6 DEAN — 7 DOYLE

13 SWALES

11 HEPWORTH — 12 COLE or ROSE

10 KIRK — 9 WAKEFIELD — 8 GOODYEAR

Brookhouse v Doncaster teams 1962

In 1963, a season disrupted by one of the worst winters in recent history, both of the junior versus senior ties were very close. Liverpool City was struggling near the bottom of the new second division and, while they were expected to beat Roose from Barrow, most pundits assumed that the juniors would provide a stiff challenge. The tie was played at Widnes on a pitch that had been treated with chemicals in order to make it playable. The decision to play at Widnes was rewarded with an attendance of 3,050. Roose battled hard throughout but they kept losing field position when they conceded penalties. The 11 points to nil score reflects just how tight the game was. The other junior club York Imperial

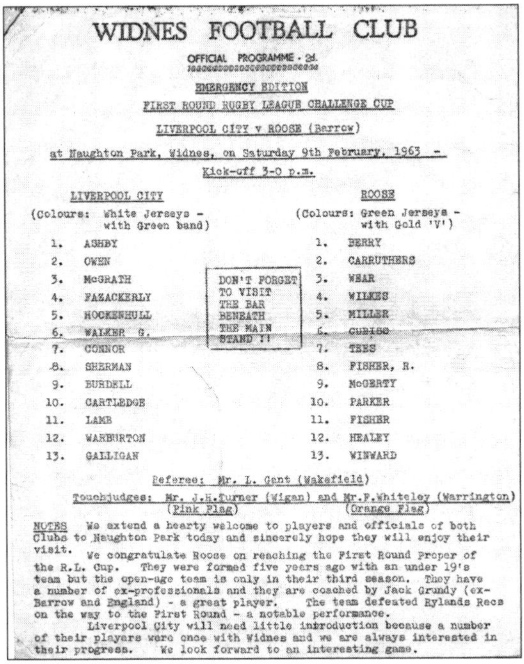

WIDNES FOOTBALL CLUB

OFFICIAL PROGRAMME - 2d.

EMERGENCY EDITION

FIRST ROUND RUGBY LEAGUE CHALLENGE CUP

LIVERPOOL CITY v ROOSE (Barrow)

at Naughton Park, Widnes, on Saturday 9th February, 1963 -

Kick-off 3-0 p.m.

LIVERPOOL CITY	ROOSE
(Colours: White Jerseys - with Green band)	(Colours: Green Jerseys - with Gold 'V')
1. ASHBY	1. BERRY
2. OWEN	2. CARRUTHERS
3. McGRATH	3. WEAR
4. FAZACKERLY	4. WILKES
5. HOCKENHULL	5. MILLER
6. WALKER G.	6. CUBISS
7. CONNOR	7. TEES
8. SHERMAN	8. FISHER, R.
9. BURDELL	9. McGERTY
10. CARTLEDGE	10. PARKER
11. LAMB	11. FISHER
12. WARBURTON	12. HEALEY
13. GALLIGAN	13. WINWARD

DON'T FORGET TO VISIT THE BAR BENEATH THE MAIN STAND !!

Referee: Mr. L. Gant (Wakefield)

Touchjudges: Mr. J.H.Turner (Wigan) (Pink Flag) and Mr.F.Whiteley (Warrington) (Orange Flag)

NOTES We extend a hearty welcome to players and officials of both Clubs to Naughton Park today and sincerely hope they will enjoy their visit.

We congratulate Roose on reaching the First Round Proper of the R.L. Cup. They were formed five years ago with an under 19's team but the open-age team is only in their third season. They have a number of ex-professionals and they are coached by Jack Grundy (ex-Barrow and England) - a great player. The team defeated Rylands Recs on the way to the First Round - a notable performance.

Liverpool City will need little introduction because a number of their players were once with Widnes and we are always interested in their progress. We look forward to an interesting game.

Liverpool City v Roose programme 1963

had a very difficult task just to reach the first round proper. They had progressed fairly comfortably through the qualifying rounds but then had to face Huddersfield club Moldgreen in the final qualifier and this was when the weather intervened. The game at Moldgreen was postponed nine times before finally taking place on the chemically treated pitch at Widnes. In a very tough game, York Imperial just had the edge and the win saw them rewarded with a home tie against first division Bramley. The game against Bramley was also affected by the weather and after two postponements it eventually took place on a Monday afternoon at York's Clarence Street ground. There were 2,684 spectators present to witness an inspired Imperial performance. Tough tackling and good covering restricted Bramley's ability to score with many of the spectators suggesting that had Imperial given that performance against a second division club they would have probably won. Bramley will have been another relieved senior outfit when they stood to applaud Imperial as they left the field at the end of the game.

It was 1966 first round when the next two close games took place. Barrow just scraped past Crosfields from Warrington, by 11 points to 2 in a tie played on a very heavy pitch that probably suited the juniors. Crosfields matched their senior opponents in all aspects of the game and, had they taken their opportunities, could have been giant killers. Brookhouse again provided a tough challenge to senior opponents Widnes only losing by 23 points to 5 in front of an impressive 6,204 spectators. The following year saw another of the increasingly rare occasions that a junior club staged a cup tie on their own ground. BOCM, from Hull, were drawn at home to Liverpool City and chose to play at home rather than switch the game to Liverpool as that would probably have produced a very small attendance and a financial loss for both clubs. Neither of the professional grounds in Hull was available as both Hull and Hull Kingston Rovers were at home and so BOCM roped off their pitch and charged the 1,566 spectators an entrance fee. The match receipts only totalled £194 so it may well be that a number of spectators found other ways to get into the ground without paying. BOCM, playing in red shirts they had borrowed from Hull Kingston

Action from BOCM v Liverpool City 1967

Rovers, took an early lead when Bob Colgrave kicked a penalty and, with Liverpool City only leading by 5 points to 4 at the interval, a shock looked possible. However, in the second half Liverpool City made good use of the wind, and with extra pace on the wings pressed home their advantage to win the game by 20 points to 9. Dennis Oaten, who was a substitute that day, recalls that BOCM were very confident going into the game. Dennis came onto the field when one of the backs was injured and made a break early in the second half that should have resulted in a try. Had it been scored it would have given BOCM the lead and put Liverpool under real pressure. However, it wasn't to be, but it did begin a run of appearances for BOCM in the Challenge Cup first round. The other junior versus senior tie in 1967 was also closely fought between Blackbrook, from St Helens, and York. The juniors were in contention right up to the 70th minute of the game that was played on the St Helens ground and watched by 6,414 spectators. Five goals from Blackbrook's twenty year old centre Johnny Houghton kept them in the tie that York only won with three late tries.

BOCM continued their Cup exploits the following year when they were drawn at home against high flying Castleford. Bob Colgrave, a leading player for BOCM during this successful period, recalls that the

BOCM v Liverpool City 1967

game was played at Castleford as again neither of the Hull professional grounds was available and it was felt that BOCM's ground would not be suitable to host a tie that could potentially attract a large crowd. Bob said that BOCM initially tried to persuade Castleford to play the game at one of Hull professional club grounds on a Sunday but they refused. The tie therefore had to take place at Castleford and again, as happened in many junior versus senior clashes, ended with a score that did not reflect the game. As Bob Colgrave recalls, BOCM received a standing ovation as they left the field at half time, having matched Castleford and only behind by 11 points to 6. However, in the second half Castleford's skill, fitness and pace told as they ran out comfortable winners. Leigh Miners Welfare were also involved in a close game in 1968 only losing by 24 points to 7 in a tie switched to Halifax. How much closer would it have been had Leigh Miners played on their home ground we will never know, but Halifax must have had an advantage playing in front of their own supporters.

In 1969 there were heavy defeats for the two junior clubs as Leigh Miners Welfare lost 61 points to nil when they visited Wigan and Ackworth made the short journey to Belle Vue to play Wakefield

Trinity losing by 50 points to 7. However, in the first round in 1970 the games were much closer. Doncaster scraped home by 22 points to 4 against Cumbrian club Glasson Rangers while Huddersfield had a real struggle against Castleford junior's Lock Lane. Huddersfield's pitch was frozen on the Saturday the game was scheduled to be played and so the following Wednesday, after a quick thaw that had left a very heavy pitch, the game took place in front of 2,366 spectators. The score at half time was 15 points to 10, and towards the end of the tie Lock Lane were the team pressing their opponents' line in the hope of scoring the converted try that would have given them a draw. However, Huddersfield just managed to hold out and the final whistle resulted in Lock Lane leaving the field with the cheers of the crowd ringing in their ears.

The 1970 Challenge Cup saw BOCM's final appearance in the first round proper when they played Dewsbury in a tie switched to the professional club's Crown Flatt ground. Dewsbury established a half time lead of 15 points to nil and were expected to coast home, but BOCM came out fired up in the second half and really stretched the home team. Dennis Oaten scored an unconverted try for the visitors and had the score remained at 15 points to 3, it would probably have reflected the effort and commitment put in by BOCM. However, Dewsbury's fitness told in the end and they scored two converted tries to seal the win.

Huddersfield v Lock Lane programme 1970

Do you care about your appearance?

so do

HUDDERSFIELD LAUNDRY

and

MOORLAND CLEANERS

WIGGAN LANE, SHEEPRIDGE

Telephone Hudds. 30384

For the "EXCLUSIVE" 3 Day Service

Branches:—
13 New North Road, Huddersfield
20 Upperhead Row, Huddersfield
1 Rashcliffe Hill Road, Huddersfield
103 Lidget Street, Lindley
Market Place, Meltham
10 Church Street, Rastrick

VAN COLLECTIONS ALL DISTRICTS

GEORGE GRAHAM'S SONS & CO. LTD.

BUILDING & MASONRY CONTRACTORS

TOM LANE
CROSLAND HILL
Tel: HUDDERSFIELD 53152

★

Any type of Building work undertaken

Sand; Stone walling; Crazy paving; Concrete flags; and Concrete edgings supplied in any quantity

Telephone: NIGHT 20988

Fartown Funeral Service

Telephone: DAY 29929

(Cremations) FARTOWN JOINERS (Embalming)
(H. G. LYNES)

ALL TYPES OF JOINERY — — SHOP-FITTERS

WORKS REAR
316, Bradford Road, Fartown Bar

Residence:
21 DAISY ROYD
NEWSOME

All round Huddersfield——READYMIX Phone 27285

HUDDERSFIELD
1 WALLACE
2 MAJOR
3 STARKEY (capt.)
4 PICKUP
5 SENIOR
6 LEEK
7 LOXTON
8 VAN BELLEN
9 CLOSE
10 DAVIES
11 VALENTINE
12 LONG
13 TAYLOR
Substitutes
14 BREAKSPEARE
15 HINCHCLIFFE

Referee:
Mr. R. WOOD
(Barrow)

HANSON FOR ALL TOUR TRAVEL

Touch Judges:
Mr. G. Thorpe
(Red Flag)
Mr. G. T. Ashton
(Yellow Flag)

LOCK LANE
1 POXTON
2 SWINSON
3 B. WALSH
4 SPARGO
5 HANSON
6 WATSON
7 PYCROFT
8 LANE
9 MARTIN
10 APPLEYARD
11 J. WALSH
12 CROSSLAND
13 TAYLOR (capt.)
Substitutes
14 PEARCE
15 WHITE

All round Huddersfield——READYMIX Phone 27285

All round Huddersfield——READYMIX Phone 27285

All round Huddersfield——READYMIX Phone 27285

DIAMONDS
WATCHES
SILVER WARE

Family Jewellers since 1852

Fillans

MARKET WALK - HUDDERSFIELD

Woodrow, Christy and Stetson Hats

Maenson, Simpson, Daks and Simon Ackerman Clothes

Burberry & Aquascutum Raincoats

Ernest Clough LTD.

Hatters, Hosiers and Shirtmakers

WESTGATE HOUSE

WESTGATE . HUDDERSFIELD

Telephone 22341

Hire Service, Day or Evening

Supplier to Engineering, Textile Works
British Forces, Hospitals, etc.

Telephone 31370
Established 1880

N. HOPKINSON LTD.

CHINA and HARDWARE MERCHANTS

ASPLEY PLACE
HUDDERSFIELD

Agent for
ROYAL DOULTON, SPODE,
SHELLEY, TUSCAN, ADAMS, etc.

Canteen Crockery a Speciality

Excellent selections of Dinner and Tea Sets

Huddersfield v Lock Lane 1970 Teams

Dewsbury Celtic and Pilkington Recreation were the two junior clubs taking part in the 1972 Challenge Cup and both gave excellent accounts of themselves, Dewsbury Celtic in particular. Celtic were drawn at home to Featherstone Rovers and in a game played on Dewsbury's ground put in a solid performance despite losing by 34 points to 2. Pilkington Recreation had to travel to struggling Bramley and had opportunities to win the tie, but in the end it was Bramley's greater experience that saw them progress to round two with a 19 points to 5 victory.

At the beginning of this chapter I describe this period as 'the barren years', mainly because of the lack of interest shown by the RFL in the junior game. I also believe that the 'luck of the draw' was a big factor. During the barren years, a number of the one-sided games happened when junior clubs drew the more successful senior outfits. The close games were when Doncaster, Liverpool City and Bramley, drew junior opposition and probably reflected the weakness of the senior club rather than the strength of the juniors. Although many of the games were one-sided, they still attracted reasonable attendances such as in 1957 when Barrow played Wakefield Loco in front of 5,123 spectators, and Halifax attracted 8,646 spectators to Thrum Hall for their tie against Widnes St Maries. In 1959, the attendance of 3,608 at York when they played Astley and Tyldesley Colliery, and the 4,078 at Hunslet who entertained Kells, would certainly have delighted those clubs today, as sadly both usually attract home attendances of less than a thousand.

Chapter 7

Amateurs v Professionals

In all the previous chapters I have called the clubs involved in the Challenge Cup either junior or senior. From this chapter on, and following the formation of the British Amateur Rugby League Association, I going to refer to the two types of clubs as amateur or professional rather than junior and senior. (In reality, after the Second World War although the vast majority of the junior clubs were amateur some did continue to pay their players.) When BARLA was formed the rules concerning a player's amateur status were clarified. However, the clubs that continued to make payments to their players did so in a variety of ways. In some cases the payment was to the coach who would probably also play. But there were some players at the leading clubs who received 'boot money', that is of course an unofficial payment. Sometimes the money came from a sponsor or in other cases from a surplus on bar takings. In the early years of the Northern Union the practice of paying players at junior clubs was made possible by the fact that many of the clubs were relatively well supported and took a gate at their home games. As spectator support for the junior clubs declined so did their ability to pay players. However, there were ambitious junior clubs that, on occasion, offered cash inducements to players to move from neighbouring clubs. At some of the more successful junior outfits, the added incentive for players was that they were not required to pay an annual subscription or a weekly match fee when they played. The costs involved in running the club were covered by fund raising or a by a donation from a sponsor. However, at many of the smaller junior clubs the only way that they could operate was if the players made a financial contribution every week. So, even though there is evidence that payments were being made to players, after 1973 the junior clubs were universally described as amateur.

Millom 1973

Following the formation of BARLA, results in the first round games involving amateur clubs did not immediately improve to the extent that the 'age of the giant killers' returned. However, Hunslet did struggle to overcome Millom in 1973 in one of the last ties to be played on an amateur club's home ground. There were 2,565 spectators at Devonshire Road, in Millom, to witness a game played at a very fast pace with the amateurs dominating the first half. Ken Sykes, who played in the second row for Hunslet, recalls what a tough encounter it was. He said '*Millom were a very physical side full of experienced players*'. When Millom led by 5 points to nil early in the game Ken remembers thinking that Hunslet were going to have to really raise their game or they going to be beaten. In the end it was the experience of Hunslet's 39 year player coach, Geoff Gunney, which proved the difference as he led from the front in

Match day ticket

Hunslet's much improved second half performance.

The 1974 qualifiers, Kippax White Swan at Leigh, and Lock Lane at Wigan, both suffered heavy defeats but then for the next seven years there were very few 'one-sided' games, even in some cases when an amateur club drew one of the top professional sides. In 1975 Hunslet drew amateurs Mayfield in their reincarnation as New Hunslet. The Rochdale club came very close to causing an upset on the narrow pitch at Hunslet's new home, the Elland Road Greyhound Stadium. Mayfield were leading by 5 points to 3 early in the second half, when they had their hooker sent off. Hunslet made their numerical advantage count as they scored two late tries to win the game. Dewsbury Celtic's tie played at Batley against Hull Kingston Rovers was not quite as close but the fifteen points Celtic scored was, at the time, the highest score by an amateur/junior club against professional's in the Challenge Cup. Celtic put up a tremendous second half performance but Rovers had established a good lead and were able to qualify comfortably for the next round.

Hunslet v Mayfield programme 1975

In 1976 Leigh Miners Welfare came close to providing a shock result when, in front of 4,285 spectators at Wilderspool, they led Warrington by 12 points to 11 with

Our Visitors . . .

When the draw for the cup was made very few people in our area had heard of our visitors Mayfield. They come from Rochdale and are one of the strongest amateur teams in Lancashire. They are on the door step of Rochdale Hornets and are regarded as one of the most progressive of junior clubs in the county. They come to us today, having survived several preliminary rounds of the competition, full of enthusiasm, and have approached their task with a real professional attitude. They watched us at Oldham and against Hull K.R. and will certainly know our weaknesses and we hope will have noticed our strengths. We have paid them the compliment of watching them. We would ask you to watch carefully for their loose forward and winger, Miller and Power. Several of their players have had professional careers and our skipper was pleased to see amongst their ranks an old team mate of his, Riley. We know that they will be all out to show their capabilities. They will want to be the first amateur team to go into the second round. It is of course a hard task but they have players of skill and ability and their team work and organisation is excellent. We would ask all our supporters to give them a special cheer when they come onto the field today and ask you to give your usual warm reception to their supporters who have made the journey. We welcome them most heartily, and we hope they will enjoy their day of glory. We hope that they go from strength to strength though obviously we do not want them to win, we wish them all good fortune in the future. We have arranged to entertain their players and officials after the match and we hope that the wounds of the losers and the joy of the victors will still make it a convivial evening. Those of our friends from Mayfield may well wish to stay over for the greyhounds race meeting and if they do we hope that they win a "few bob." We would not recommend them to follow any of the tips given by one of our directors, who shall be nameless. To the lads of Mayfield then, a warm welcome and a happy and enjoyable day. ■

Hunslet v Mayfield 1975 Our Vistors

just a few minutes remaining. Derek Whitehead saved Warrington's blushes when he scored a late try that he also converted. The match report in the Warrington Guardian praised the amateurs and suggested that as they played much better football than Warrington they should have won the tie. Pointer Panthers, the Castleford amateurs did not fare quite so well at Leigh, losing by 37 points to 8.

The amateur clubs involved in 1977 certainly provided very stiff opposition. Beecroft and Whiteman played Swinton at Hull's Boulevard ground in front of 4,186 spectators and put up a great performance in losing by 10 points to 2. With a half time score of 2-2 the game was in the balance. Swinton did not finally seal the victory until their scrum half Jimmy Green scored a try converted by full back Jeff Gorton. The other tie played at Knowlsley Road, between Pilkington Recreation and Wigan, produced the largest attendance at the ground that season. 11,000 spectators saw a very close game with the professionals finding it difficult to establish any sort of superiority, eventually winning by 10 points to 4. The following year, 1978, Wigan again drew amateur opposition away and perhaps, because of their experience the previous year, tried to persuade their opponents Dewsbury Celtic to switch the tie. Celtic agreed to switch providing Wigan paid them £1,500 in compensation. However, Wigan only offered £1,000 initially, a figure that was increased to £1,250 and then finally £1,500, but by that stage Celtic said they had incurred costs of over £500 already and refused the offer. The game, set to be staged on Batley's Mount Pleasant ground, was initially postponed on its scheduled date, and then re-arranged for a Wednesday afternoon with a 3.30pm kick off. Despite the game being in mid-week and with an afternoon kick off over 4,000 spectators were in attendance. The Wigan coach Vince Karalius said after the game that his club was very lucky to win. It was noted in the match report in the Yorkshire Post that the only difference between the teams was Wigan's extra pace. The other first round tie produced not only a nail biting contest but also another excellent attendance as 7,600 spectators, at Knowlsley Road, saw Pilkington Recreation lose 23 points to 22 to Castleford. The St Helens amateurs had gone into the game full of confidence. Their performance against Wigan the previous year had convinced the players that they were a match for any professional club. Pilkington's raced into an early lead and it was only a try, just before half time by Castleford's winger Steve Fenton that kept them in contention. Pilkington's led their professional opponents by 20 points to 13 at half time and, although Castleford managed to score two converted tries in the second half to edge in front, Pilkington's continued to play open football closing to within a point of the West Yorkshire club.

After the two close results in 1978, the next two years saw the professionals tested but never really in danger of losing. Leigh Miners Welfare drew their professional neighbours Leigh in 1979 to set up an intriguing local derby. The tie, that attracted an attendance of over 8,000, saw Leigh Miners put up a great performance. They led by 7 points to 3 after fourteen minutes and although Leigh hit back to lead 11 points to 7 at the interval; it wasn't until the last ten minutes that the professional outfit were able to establish a winning lead. However, Leigh Miners never gave up and continued to battle right to the end with winger John Roberts scoring an unconverted try in the final minute. Leigh's greater experience and the skills of stand – off John Woods saw them win the pulsating tie by 23 points to 13. Ace Amateurs, from Hull, qualified for the first round proper in 1979 and played Oldham in a tie that was postponed five times and eventually had to be played at Salford's ground on a Wednesday evening. Unfortunately, the Ace Amateurs coach broke down on the motorway and the players arrived twenty minutes before kick-off. Despite their disrupted preparations Ace were only 5 points to nil down after thirty nine minutes but then conceded a try in the final minute of the half and one in the first minute of the second half. Oldham had taken control of the game and went on to win by 23 points to 5. It was exactly the same score in 1980 when Ace played Widnes on Hull's Boulevard ground. In the other tie Hull proved too strong for Cumbrian amateurs Millom winning by 33 points to 10.

Hull v Millom Programme 1980

In 1981 only one club made up the numbers and that was Pilkington Recreation. Ironically, with only one amateur club in the Cup, the sponsors State Express offered £5,550 to the first amateur club to beat professional opponents. Pilkington's were confident of winning the prize when they entertained York at Knowlsley Road in front of an impressive 5,694 attendance. The 18 points to 7 victory by York was

Bankers: Midland — Payment: Cash or Cheque

'BASSETTS OF HULL'

(REGISTERED METAL MERCHANTS)

Office & Works:

169 FOUNTAIN ROAD

Telephone 23245

TOP BUYERS OF

BRASS, COPPER, LEAD ETC.

WE ARE OPEN OVER LUNCH. DAILY COLLECTIONS.

For rings watches and all types of the finest jewellery

HENRY HIRD'S The Jewellers OF 270 HESSLE ROAD. HULL. Tel. 24640

ART WELLS

ROSSY BROTHERS

WHERE SPORT BEGINS

Telephone 51272

Today's MITRE BALL donated by TONY SHEARS

HULL — Black and White Irregular Hoops

MILLOM — Maroon Shirts with white 'V' white shorts

HULL	No.	Position	No.	MILLOM
PAUL WOODS	1	Full Back	1	P. KNOWLES
PAUL PRENDIVILLE	2	Right Wing	2	M. JAMES
GRAHAM WALTERS	3	Right Centre	3	J. BAWDEN
GRAHAM EVANS	4	Left Centre	4	R. MORRIS
S. DENNISON	5	Left Wing	5	I. JAMES
JOHN NEWLOVE	6	Stand Off	6	C. MOSSOP
CLIVE PICKERILL	7	Scrum Half	7	P. DATE
KEITH TINDALL	8	Field Prop	8	J. JACKSON
RON WILEMAN	9	Hooker	9	T. CLARKSON
CHARLIE STONE	10	Blind Prop	10	S. FALLOWS
C. Birdsall/K. Boxall	11	Second Row	11	J. LUPTON
SAMMY LLOYD	12	Second Row	12	P. SWALES
STEVE NORTON	13	Loose Forward	13	S. MOSSOP
	14	Substitute	14	S. CUMMINGS
	15	Substitute	15	N. DAWSON

Referee: J. McDONALD (Wigan)

Touch Judges: A. I. BARROW, F. M. LOFTHOUSE

Allsports

SUPPLIERS TO HULL F.C.

FOOTBALL, RUGBY, CRICKET, SWIMMING, HOCKEY, CAMPING, TENNIS, WEIGHT-LIFTING, BADMINTON, GOLF, SQUASH, BOXING, ATHLETICS · SNOOKER · BILLIARDS · DARTS

FERENSWAY HULL Telephone 29289

HULL DAILY MAIL and SPORTS MAIL

First with all the Rugby League news on Humberside

Modern or traditional you will find everything for your home and at BARGAIN PRICES TOO! So why not score for your interior?

GOLDSTONES 16-22 Anlaby Rd. Hull Tel. 225383

Late Night Friday until 6.30 p.m.

FRED LORD LTD. Telephone 20324

... Pays Cash for Scrap

ALL GRADES OF FERROUS AND NON FERROUS METALS

8 ETON STREET - HESSLE ROAD - HULL

YOU'LL SCORE EVERY TIME WITH THE CLOTHING HOUSE (HESSLE ROAD)

PREMIER ARMY STORES

THE CHAMPION WRANGLER AND DOC MARTIN STOCKIST

If you are reading this programme now 'YOU MUST BE THE CREAM'

So we invite you to shop with us and have a 10% cash discount. Answer one quiz question on HULL F.C. correctly and you get a 20% discount.

That is of course everyone except the referee.

64 Carr Lane. 361 Hessle Rd. 152/4 Hessle Rd. 357 Holderness Rd.

Hull v Millom 1980 Teams

just about deserved in a game marred by constant penalties many of which were given to the amateurs. York complained that the referee influenced the game, but will have been relieved at the final whistle to have qualified for the next round.

It is not clear whether the Cup sponsors State Express realised that they were very unlikely, with just one amateur club involved, to ever pay out the £5,550 prize money. However, what is certain is that no amateur club would be able to beat a professional club in the Challenge Cup for the next four years as no amateurs were required to make up the numbers. The consolation for the amateur clubs was a place in the John Player Trophy. This early season knockout competition, later to become the Regal Trophy, was first played for in 1971. Amateur clubs were included in the competition on a similar basis to the Challenge Cup mainly to make up the numbers. Over the years the number of amateur's that had been invited to take part in the John Player Trophy had increased and in later years they were joined in the draw by some of the French professional clubs. However, as the John Player/Regal Trophy was generally regarded as much less prestigious than the Challenge Cup, the involvement in that competition of more amateur clubs certainly did not make up for their absence from the Challenge Cup. The loss of amateur clubs from the Challenge Cup was an issue that BARLA fought very hard on until, in 1986, the amateur clubs were allowed back in the Challenge Cup and Dudley Hill and Kells took part in the preliminary round. I have no doubt that BARLA regarded the inclusion of amateur clubs in the Cup as a victory, fully justifying the lobbying that had taken place since 1982. In 1986 there were thirty four clubs in the professional ranks and so the two amateur clubs and six professional clubs took part in an eight club preliminary round. The professional clubs that took part in the preliminary round were not seeded and so three first division and three second outfits joined the amateurs. Neither Dudley Hill nor Kells looked like beating their professional opponents although Kells did get within twelve points of Hunslet when they lost by 20 points to 8.

The following year, 1987, Kells built on the experience gained playing Hunslet when they held second division Fulham to a 4-4 draw in a gripping preliminary round tie at Whitehaven, but then lost 22 points to 14 in the replay. It had been seventy eight years since a senior/professional club had been beaten by a junior/amateur club in a straight knockout round of the Challenge Cup. Was the gap closing? It certainly appeared to be, off the field, if what happened in the Mansfield Marksman versus Heworth first round tie is an indication. Heworth had reached the first round by beating fellow amateurs Elland by 10 points to 6 at Halifax. As soon the draw for the first round was made Heworth offered Mansfield £500 to switch the tie to York and also offered to pay £100 to hire a coach to bring Mansfield's supporters to the game. This remarkable offer, probably the first time a junior/amateur club had ever offered to host senior/professional opponents on the basis that there would be a greater attendance, was turned down by Mansfield. After an initial postponement the tie was scheduled for Mansfield's home ground Alfreton Town soccer club on a Thursday evening. The game was very close and it was only an inspired performance from Mansfield full back

14(2) 7(4)

MARKSMAN V HEWORTH

Colours: Light Blue & Dark Blue Shirts, Dark Blue Shorts with Gold trim.

Colours: Black & White hooped Shirts. Black Shorts

PAUL TOPPING 2gls + 2dg's	1 (Full Back)	JIM CURRY
ANDY FLETCHER 2t	2 (Right Wing)	ANDREW TINDALL
~~COLIN FLETCHER~~ DAVE EDMISTON	3 (Right Centre)	DAVID MEEK
~~SHANE TUPAEA (CAPT.)~~ TONY COCHRANE	4 (Left Centre)	3gls N. RENNISON
COURTNEY THOMPSON	5 (Left Wing)	~~N. DOLLING~~/A. MERCER
CHRIS WILLIS	6 (Stand Off)	CARL DEIGHTON
TERRY LANGTON	7 (Scrum Half)	1dg. CHRIS HAMMERTON (CAPT
~~WAYNE GRIX~~ NEIL KELLETT	8 (Openside Prop)	KEN SYKES
DARREN STEVENS	9 (Hooker)	JIM WEST
~~MICK HOUGH~~ CRAIG WHITEHEAD	10 (Blindside Prop)	STEPHEN O' GORMAN
~~CRAIG WHITEHEAD~~ WAYNE GRIX	11 (2nd Row Forward)	IAN PAVER
~~ANDY DUFFY~~ JOHN BUCKTON	12 (2nd Row Forward)	KEITH LOFT
~~JOHN BUCKTON~~ SHANE TUPAEA	13 (Loose Forward)	PHIL STURDY
BARRY HOLDEN	14 (Substitute)	IAN ELLIS (DEIGHTON)
~~NEIL KELLETT~~ PETER BLACKMORE (KELLETT)	15 (Substitute)	COLIN FORSYTH (SYKES)

REFEREE: John Mean (Leyland)
TOUCH JUDGES: PM Oliver(Horwich)
GE Lightfoot (Bolton)

Today's Match Sponsors
SILK CUT

Mansfield v Heworth team sheet 1987

Paul Topping that ensured the professionals won the game. Ken Sykes, who played for Hunslet against Millom in 1973, had returned to play for his amateur club Heworth and remembers how disappointed the Heworth players were at the end of the game. They were convinced that they had more than matched their professional opponents and should have won. However, the good performance by Heworth, on the field, was marred by controversy off it. The attendance was announced at 701 but many of the spectators that attended, particularly those from

York, believed that the attendance was at least 1,200, and as Heworth's gatemen were not allowed to check the turnstiles perhaps they were right. Heworth did not complain about the attendance figure as they felt a complaint might sound like 'sour grapes' because they had lost the game on the field. However, what this tie indicates was that a number of amateur clubs were probably in a better shape financially and in some cases better supported than some of the professional clubs. In that sense the gap had probably narrowed.

Back row (L-R) Barry Jackson (Trustee), Geoff Garvey (Assistant Coach), Neil Rennison, Paul West, Carl Deighton, Andy Tindall, John Kemp Keith Loft, Dave Meek, Ian Paver, Ken SYkes, Paul Smith, Colin Forsyth, Geoff Taylor, (Harris Bacon, Heworth's Sponsor).

Front Row (L-R0 Steve O' Gorman, Graham Walkinson, Mark Forsyth, Chris Hammerton, Ian Ellis, Phil Sturdy, John Young, Terry Roberts (kitman), Richard Gray (Chairman).

Heworth 1987

Over the next few years the dramatic events of 1987 both on and off the field were not repeated. However, in 1989 Thatto Heath from St Helens came very close to knocking out Chorley Borough, losing by only 8 points to 4. Similarly, in 1991 Hensingham put up a very brave performance, at Workington, against Dewsbury. The professionals won the game with a three try scoring burst in just twelve minutes late in the first half and early in the second. For the other sixty eight minutes Hensingham were the better team and deserved the standing ovation from the 1,067 crowd as they left the field at the end of the game. The following year, 1992, Kells pushed third division Hunslet all the way and the professionals needed a fourteen point scoring burst in the last twelve minutes to make the game safe. The tie attracted 1,107 spectators to a freezing Whitehaven ground on a Wednesday night, possibly a bigger attendance than had the game been played at Hunslet.

There was no amateur involvement in the 1993 Challenge Cup as a major re-organisation of the way the competition was structured was about to take place. In 1993, with thirty five professional clubs playing in three divisions, there were just six professional clubs in the preliminary round. Three clubs needing to be eliminated in order to give thirty two clubs in the first round draw. Playing in the preliminary round was not a very attractive proposition for any of the professional outfits and it could well have been motivation for the changes that took place to the format of the 1994 Challenge Cup competition.

Chapter 8

Underprepared

The Challenge Cup format underwent a dramatic change in 1994. Gone were the preliminary rounds that had been a feature of the competition since 1982 and, after they had been allowed back into the Challenge Cup, had included amateur clubs from 1986. The qualifying competition that had often stretched to seven or eight rounds and been a feature of the Cup since the beginning of the century had disappeared in 1973 when BARLA was formed. The amateur clubs that had been allowed into the Cup after the formation of BARLA were usually the winners of the County cup competitions from the previous season or, in some years, the qualifiers came from a play off between the County cup winners.

In 1994 the amateur clubs that took part in the Cup were selected from the leading National Conference League (NCL) clubs. Those amateur clubs began the competition in the first round and the winners played a second round before been put into the third round draw with the sixteen second division clubs. However, it wasn't an open draw in the third round as all the professional clubs were given home advantage. Very few, if any, amateur clubs were able to stage a Cup game against a professional club on their home ground. The days of roping off your pitch so that you could play on a local park, as happened in 1962 when Brookhouse played Doncaster were long gone, as was the ability to cram over 2,500 spectators into a tiny ground with no real spectator facilities or permanent covered areas as happened in 1973 when Millom played Hunslet.

The NCL was created by BARLA as the 'flagship' amateur competition, a means of raising standards amongst the leading amateur clubs both on and off the field. The NCL had criteria regarding facilities, playing strength and junior development. In order to join the NCL, a club had to demonstrate that it met the standards required on and off the field and also that it was committed to maintaining those standards. By 1994 many of the NCL clubs had developed their facilities with the majority having enclosed grounds including some with covered stands and floodlights. This meant that many of the NCL clubs were possibly in a better financial position than a number of the professional clubs. The RFL had 'courted' the NCL for a number of years hoping to persuade the league to leave BARLA and come under the control of the RFL. If that had happened it would have given the RFL a group of successful clubs operating below the professional divisions, a competition that could possibly accommodate some of the less successful professional sides. In 1994, if a professional club was struggling unless its fortunes improved both on and off the field the only option for that club was to fold. Perhaps some of the decision makers at the RFL had looked at the league structure in soccer where clubs can be relegated from the Football League into the 'non-league' competition with the opportunity, if their fortunes revived, of being promoted back into the Football League. When three RFL clubs, Blackpool Gladiators, Chorley Borough and Nottingham City, had been relegated from the third division at the end of the 1992/93 season they were given a place in the NCL. However, because the RFL did not govern the NCL, there were issues that could not be easily resolved regarding integrating a professional club into an amateur competition. The clubs in the NCL were, understandably, unhappy that three clubs that paid their players were to join their league. The three relegated clubs were equally unhappy at being placed in a competition where their ability to revive their fortunes was affected by an inability to attract the good players needed in order to improve their playing standards. Also the loss of gate income from playing against NCL clubs that on a good day attracted a few hundred people to their home games, and had virtually no travelling support, was not going to help revive the fortunes of a club in financial difficulties. The clubs that were relegated did not survive very long and certainly did not use the NCL as a stepping stone back into the professional game. Whether the decision to welcome large numbers of NCL clubs, and later some clubs from other amateur leagues, into the Challenge Cup was part of a plan to encourage the leading amateur clubs to leave BARLA is not documented. However, the fact that so many additional clubs were invited into the Challenge Cup at a time when relations between BARLA and RFL were at an all-time low must be significant!

Whatever the reasons were for the re-structuring of the Cup in 1994, the majority of the sixteen amateur clubs that took part in the third round were well beaten. There were only two games where the professional club did not score at least thirty points and they were at Workington Town, where the hosts beat Beverley by 24 points to 10, and at Highfield where the professional club beat Saddleworth by 16 points to 13 in a game that the Oldham amateurs should have won. The attendances at all of the games were very disappointing, often numbering a few hundred. Only two attendances reached four figures. Keighley versus Oulton attracted 2,210 and Workington Town's tie against Beverley had an attendance of 1,277. The very poor attendances must have raised some concerns and questions about the value of all the professional clubs in the third round being given home advantage when they faced amateur opposition. However, if concerns were raised they were ignored, as the following season all the professional clubs were again given home advantage. A practice that continued until 2002, apart from when amateur clubs drew French opponents.

The third round in 1995 produced its share of one-sided games. Dewsbury's seventy two points against Kells was the highest score but there were also six other ties where the professional club scored fifty or more points. It was therefore surprising that, in a year when many of the third round scores seemed to indicate that the gap in playing standards between amateurs and professionals was continuing to widen, we should see the return of the giant killers. Ironically, it was a Beverley club that performed the giant killing act, beating Highfield by 27 points to 4. The irony, of course, was that it was a Beverley club in 1909 that were the last giant killers. Whether the club that existed in 1909 is the same club that was playing in 1995 is difficult to prove. Rugby league had not been played consistently in the town during the Twentieth Century but, as in 1909, the club that performed the giant killing act was called 'Beverley'. The Beverley victory at Highfield wasn't altogether unexpected. In 1994 Beverley had given Workington Town a very tough game before losing, and of course Highfield had only won by three points when they played Saddleworth Rangers. Highfield had struggled both on and off the field for the previous two seasons and in fact only managed one league win in the whole of the 1994/95 season. However, despite their very poor league form Highfield, with home advantage, were expected to beat their amateur opponents. In reality the game was very one-sided with Beverley dominating. They led 15 points to nil at half time and were completely in control when Highfield scored their consolation try. Len Casey, a Wembley winner with Hull Kingston Rovers in 1980, coached the Beverley team that went into the draw for the fourth round full of confidence.

Beverley 1995

QUOTES FROM THE THIRD ROUND

"Indeed, it was hard to believe which side were the professionals and which were the amateurs, as Beverley gave their paid rivals an object lesson in the basics of rugby league" ST. HELENS STAR

"A magnificent performance, a real professional job, Beverley came here to win and won well" GEOFF FLETCHER, CHAIRMAN HIGHFIELD RLFC.

"Congratulations to Beverley for a magnificent performance, it is appropriate that it has come in the game's centenary year as it reflects the great strides made by BARLA.

Beverley have become the first to achieve this marvellous feat for 86 years, but I believe there are several other amateur clubs now capable of upsetting professional teams" MAURICE OLDROYD, CHIEF EXEC. BARLA

'We had a few anxious moments early doors but to be honest they're lucky we didn't stick another three or fours tries past them. That's how good we were" LEN CASEY, BEVERLEY COACH

"Not for one minute, in the lead up to the game, did I doubt the lads could do it, but to win in such style was an added bonus"
MARTIN DUNN, BEVERLEY COACH

"Indeed, such was Beverley's superiority in every phase of the game, perhaps the only disappointment was the fact they failed to bury Highfield under an even bigger avalanche of points" JOHN FIELDHOUSE, HULL DAILY MAIL

"Beverley repeated their feat of 1909 as they became the only amateurs to progress into the fourth round" THE TIMES

"Giant Killing Beverley turned the clock back 86 years when they sensationally dumped Highfield out of the Silk Cut Challenge Cup" THE DAILY STAR

"Big guns Leeds and Wigan continue to slug it out at the top of the table. But yesterday they were eclipsed By little Beverley, of the National Conference League First Division. Len Casey's Humberside underdogs became the first amateur club to defeat professional opponents in the Challenge Cup since they beat Ebbw Vale back In 1909, RUGBY LEAGUE EXPRESS

Beverley v Highfield 1995 Quotes

In the fourth round, all the clubs had an equal chance of being at home or away. Beverley were drawn at home against Batley and decided to stage the game at Hull's Boulevard ground. Batley were having a good season in the second division and were expected to have a comfortable victory over their amateur opponents but the game did not go according to expectations. With nine minutes left Beverley were leading by 20 points to 18 when the Batley half back Simon Wilson chipped through and appeared to knock on as he touched the ball down inches from the dead ball line. Unfortunately, for Beverley the referee awarded the try and then in the dying minutes Batley scored again to seal the victory. Many of the 3,275 spectators at the game were convinced that an injustice had been done and that Beverley were robbed of the opportunity to become the first junior/amateur club ever to reach the last sixteen of the Challenge Cup.

The following year an amateur club did reach the last sixteen. It had been eighty six years since the last giant killing, but Beverley's exploits in 1995 were more than matched by West Hull in 1996. Highfield were again the victims of the giant killing act, easily beaten by West Hull in the third round by 35 points to 20. West Hull had dominated from the first whistle and led 14 points to 4 at half time. Highfield only managed to make the result look a little more respectable when they scored a consolation try in injury time. In the fourth round West Hull created rugby league history by beating York. This game was played on a snow covered and frozen pitch at the Boulevard. West Hull dominated territory and possession and 1,886 spectators saw the Hull amateurs come back from losing by 6 points to 4 at half time to win the game by 10 points to 6. West Hull were brought down to earth in the fifth round by Wakefield Trinity who comfortably beat the Humbersiders by 40 points to 8 but until the 60th minute it would have been difficult to tell which was the professional team. With the score at 20 points to 8, West Hull had more than matched their opponents. However, a four try scoring burst between the 61st and the 68th minute gave Wakefield an unassailable lead. The tie was again staged at the Boulevard and attracted 4,363 spectators, adding to the income raised by the West Hull cup run which saw them bank nearly £20,000. There were no other shock results in 1996, although Heworth who played Bramley at Kirkstall, the former Headingley Rugby Union ground, in front of 1,200 spectators came close to causing an upset. The York amateurs were leading by 18 points to 16 with two minutes to go when Bramley scored a converted try to win the game. In 1996 the RFL moved its league season into the summer but continued to play the Challenge Cup rounds in the early months of the year. This meant that the amateurs were handed an unexpected advantage in the third round. The amateur clubs were still playing a winter season and so when the third round took place, usually in January, the amateurs were half way through their season while the professionals were either one or two games into the new season or just preparing to begin league fixtures. This put the 'battle hardened' amateurs at an advantage over the underprepared professionals. Many of the professional clubs would recruit new players over the close season and it often took a few competitive games for those players to fit in and 'gel' as a team. The amateurs certainly capitalised on the situation over the next few years as more and more giant killing acts followed.

In 1997 Doncaster found Oulton very tough opponents, just scraping home by 15 points to 14. A dropped goal by Doncaster's loose forward Rob Turner in the 76th minute was the decisive score. Oulton came back strongly in the closing minutes and in injury time a dropped goal attempt to level the scores by Phil Edgell just went wide. Siddal lost 16 points to 8 at Barrow in a game that was in the balance until the 78th minute. Barrow had led by 10 points to 2 at half time but when, early in the second half, Gary Lewis scored a try converted by Nicky Wood, Siddal were right back in the game. Darren Wilson scored Barrow's late try to seal the victory. Hull amateurs Skirlaugh gave Whitehaven a very tough game losing 12 points to 6. All of Skirlaugh's points came from Andy Smith who kicked three goals, but despite playing some very entertaining football Skirlaugh couldn't score the try that their efforts deserved. Alongside the close games there were also some heavy defeats for the amateurs. Whitehaven's Cumbrian neighbours Workington Town ran in eighty six points against Thatto Heath and Huddersfield scored eighty two points against East Leeds. However, pride of place in 1997 must go to Bradford club Dudley Hill. They were drawn at York and for the professionals it was a case of lightening striking twice. When they were beaten by West Hull in 1996, York could argue that the terrible weather had contributed to their defeat. Against Dudley Hill there were no such excuses. York were completely outplayed and even though Dudley Hill had to rely on a penalty from Craig Hillam ten minutes from time, which gave them a seven point lead. The reality was that York never looked like winning. Unfortunately Dudley Hill probably did not gain financially from their victory as only 647 spectators attended the game and the fourth round draw that paired them with Carlisle wasn't kind to them either. The long trip to the North West ended with a 62 points to 2 defeat in front of only 523 spectators.

The 1998 Challenge Cup produced four giant killing acts, a record number for any one year of the Cup. Doncaster, after scraping home against Oulton the previous season, found their luck had run out when they lost by 23 points to 18 to Featherstone Lions who were outstanding in the second half and finished the stronger team. A try in the 59th minute to Simon Bickerton and penalty in the 64th minute by Nick Frankland gave the amateurs a deserved victory. Ellenborough Rangers took advantage of the fact that Bramley had problems both on and off the field, to record a 16 points to 10 victory. Ellenborough's scrum half Gary Murdock ran the game and, although Bramley had the edge in power and fitness, Ellenborough showed great courage and spirit and when Paul Mc Gee kicked a penalty to extend the amateur club's lead to six points the victory was assured. The two amateurs were joined in the fourth round by Ovenden who beat Moldgreen 20 points to 10, and Egremont who had also beaten amateur opponents Eastmoor by 20 points to 16. In the fourth round all four amateur clubs were drawn at home. Ovenden played Salford at Halifax and lost 74 points to nil. Featherstone Lions were well beaten by Hull KR at Featherstone Rovers ground by 56 points to 20. The Lions seemed to be overawed by the occasion and allowed Hull Kingston Rovers to establish an early lead. They fought hard to get the score back to 12 points to 8 but then a scoring burst by Rovers gave them an unassailable 40 points to 8 half time lead. The two Cumbrian clubs, however, kept marching on. Ellenborough beat Hunslet, in a tie played at Workington Town's ground, by 14 points to 12. Ellenborough led by 10 points to 2 at half time and despite a very strong Hunslet fight back in the second half, the Cumbrians just held on. It was the professional club's lack of discipline that caused their downfall. They had two players sent off in the first half and gave away numerous penalties which meant that, throughout the game, they either conceded field position or points. Hunslet could have levelled the score in injury time when, after England International winger Ikram Butt had touched down for a try in the corner, they had a conversion attempt to draw the game. The conversion was missed and Ellenborough were through to the next round where they were joined by fellow Cumbrians Egremont. Robert Purdham, who later went on to play for London Broncos and England, was the man of the match in Egremont's convincing win over professional neighbours Workington Town. The game took place at Whitehaven's ground on a Friday evening, in front over 3,000 supporters. In beating Workington by 18 points to nil, Egremont became the first junior/amateur club to nil professional opposition for over ninety years. Egremont lead 8 points to nil at half time and could have expected a Workington fight back but it did not happen and Egremont always looked likeliest to score. This famous victory was rewarded with a trip to face the eventual cup winners Sheffield Eagles. The Super League club proved far too strong for the amateurs, racking up eighty four points in a very one-sided tie. Ellenborough's reward for reaching the fifth round was a trip to Hull where they were heavily beaten by 78 points to nil.

The 1998 Challenge Cup had been remarkable for the number of giant killing acts and so it was obviously going to be difficult for the amateurs to achieve the same level of success. In 1999. Bramley, for the second year in succession, were beaten by amateur opposition when they lost by 18 points to 12 to Leigh Miners Rangers. After being 10 points to 6 up at half time, Bramley went behind by 17 points to 12 and when, late in the game, Chris Wilkinson dropped a goal Rangers had sealed the win. Leigh Miners Rangers reward for beating Bramley was a fourth round home game against Hull Kingston Rovers. The tie was staged at Hilton Park in Leigh and 1,317 spectators saw the amateurs concede fifty two unanswered points in a game where the skill and experience of their professional opponents proved too much. The other amateur club in the fourth round was Featherstone Lions, but they reached that stage by beating fellow amateurs Hemel Hempstead 29 points to 8. In the fourth round Featherstone Lions did not fare any better than Leigh Miners Rangers, losing by 74 points to 6 against Halifax. In 1999 there could have been a third amateur club in the fourth round as Doncaster needed extra time to beat Oldham St Anne's by 35 points to 21. The score at full time was 15 -15 and the Doncaster players left the field while the St Anne's players celebrated the draw until it was realised, by the Doncaster officials, that the Challenge Cup rules had changed that season. There were no longer to be replays in Cup ties! If the scores were level at full-time twenty minutes extra time had to be played. When the Doncaster players finally returned to the field, over 500 of the 1,614 crowd had left the ground. They must have assumed that the tie would be replayed. Doncaster dominated the extra time period to record what was described in the Yorkshire Post match report as an '*ill deserved*' victory. There were some one-sided games in 1999 with Featherstone Rovers beating Thornhill Trojans by 70 points to 6 and Hunslet, York, Rochdale and Lancashire Lynx all scoring over 50 points, but in most of the other games the amateurs were competitive.

Oldham St Anne's, who had come very close to beating professional opposition in 1999, went one better in 2000 beating Batley by 10 points to nil to join the illustrious band of giant killers. In a game played in very difficult conditions, St Anne's dominated their professional opponents. David Ward, the Batley coach, said after the game '*All the ingredients were present for an upset. There was the wind, the rain, the mud and the fact that Batley had not been playing well in the run up to the match*'. However, in 2000 it was Thornhill Trojans that possibly caused the biggest shock by beating Sheffield Eagles 16 points to 14. Sheffield

Eagles, the club that won the Challenge Cup in 1998, had merged with Huddersfield Giants and so the club that Thornhill beat was not the one that had beaten Wigan at Wembley. The newly formed Sheffield Eagles were surprised by Thornhill who competed for the full eighty minutes and deserved their victory. Sheffield led by 8 points to 6 at half time but lost the lead in the 51st minute when Thornhill's substitute forward, Abe Phillips, crashed over for a try. Thornhill continued to dominate and finally sealed their win in the 68th minute when winger Barry Drummond scored. Although Sheffield fought back and scored a try three minutes from time, they could not find a way to regain the lead. Wath Brow Hornets, who beat fellow amateurs Eccles in the third round, joined the two giant killers in round four. Unfortunately, all three amateur clubs were heavily beaten in round four. Wath Brow lost 44 points to 18 at London Broncos, Oldham St Anne's switched their tie to their opponents Castleford's ground and lost by 64 points to 8, and Thornhill Trojans lost by 56 points to 2 at York. For the first time for many years a Welsh club took part in the third round of the Challenge Cup. Cardiff Cougars, a very young and inexperienced team consisting mainly of students, was heavily beaten by Keighley who scored ninety points but with a little bit of steadiness in attack could easily have scored over one hundred.

In 2001 there was just one giant killing act and it wasn't really a surprise. Woolston Rovers beat Chorley Lynx by 22 points to 8. The Warrington based amateurs went into the game full of confidence, took the lead just after half time and never looked like losing it. This was the thirtieth straight defeat suffered by the professional club. Chorley had begun life as Blackpool Borough in 1950 and over the years had changed its name and its home ground a number of times. The defeat by Woolston was one of many suffered by the club that eventually folded in 2004. Woolston's reward for beating Chorley was a fourth round tie at neighbours Warrington. The amateurs were always going to find it difficult against the full-time Super League side and the 48 points to 6 defeat was expected, although after fifty minutes and with the score at 24 points to 12 Woolston were matching their illustrious neighbours.

Woolston competed for the full eighty minutes and were disappointed with the final score that did not really reflect their efforts. However, they were rewarded by a share of an excellent 6,008 attendance. In 2001 the majority of games produced big scores for the professional clubs. There were only three ties, Oulton's 24 points to 12 defeat by York, Gateshead's 34 points to 20 victory over Wigan St Judes and Leigh's 24 points to 5 victory over West Hull where the score reflected a competitive game. Over the previous six years, the giant killing acts had usually occurred when one of the leading amateur clubs had drawn a struggling professional club. Perhaps in 2001, apart from Chorley Lynx, the best amateurs were drawn against the better professional clubs, or were the professionals becoming better prepared for a tough game in the Challenge Cup in the early part of their season?

In 2002 the professionals were no longer automatically given home advantage in the third round. This gave the amateur clubs drawn at home an opportunity to stage the tie at a suitable venue; usually their local professional club's ground. If this was an attempt to increase interest in the third round it did not have that effect. Only three attendances reached four figures. This was possibly because none of the ties in 2002 were local derbies, but also perhaps because spectator interest in the Challenge Cup was waning and attendances even in the later rounds were disappointing. 2002 was a year without giant killers. There were some close games. Swinton needed extra time to beat Skirlaugh 32 points to 24 and Redhill came close to beating Chorley Lynx, only losing by 10 points to 2 in a game that needed a try from Wayne Bloor for Chorley to seal the win. Hunslet just scraped home 18 points to 13 against Woolston having been 13 points to 8 behind at half time. The professional team had full back Kieran Allen, who kicked four penalties, and winger Gareth Naylor, who made a try saving tackle in the dying minutes, to thank for their victory.

A local derby did take place in 2003 when 3,017 spectators, at Whitehaven, saw Wath Brow Hornets beat Workington Town 13 points to 12. The Cumbrian amateurs then played Batley in the fourth round again at Whitehaven, and gave a very good performance before losing 18 points to 6. Halton Simms Cross were the other giant killers, beating new professional club London Skolars by 15 points to 8. London Skolars had led 8 points to 7 at half time but two converted tries and a dropped goal was sufficient for the Widnes amateurs to win the tie. Their reward was a trip to Wigan where 3,790 spectators saw the Super League giants win by 82 points to 3.

In 2004 there were only three really one-sided games. Featherstone Rovers beat Lock Lane 96 points to nil, Halifax played Oulton at home and won by 66 points to 10 and Elland switched their tie against Leigh to the professional club's ground and were beaten 64 points to 4. As well as the three one-sided games there were also three giant killers. Sharlston attracted 2,027 spectators to the Featherstone Rovers ground as they hosted and beat Dewsbury. Sharlston, led by player coach Martyn Wood, the Sheffield Eagles loose forward when they beat Wigan at Wembley in 1998, came from behind to win. Sharlston were probably the strongest amateur club in the country and their giant killing act wasn't unexpected. The other two clubs that beat professional opposition certainly did not approach their ties as favourites. Dudley

Sharlston Celebrations in 2004 after their victory over Dewsbury

Hill had beaten professional opposition before, but when they were drawn against Keighley the expectation was that professional club would have an easy passage into the next round. The game was switched to Keighley's ground giving the professionals an additional advantage, but Dudley Hill, led by former Keighley player Chris Robinson, gave an inspired performance, in stark contrast to Keighley's display. The professional club's players were described in the Keighley News match report as displaying '*a reckless arrogance*'. East Hull were the other giant killers easily beating Swinton by 26 points to 14. Unfortunately, none of the three amateur clubs got a 'money spinning' draw in the fourth round. 1,400 spectators at Hull Kingston Rover's ground saw East Hull come very close to causing another upset when only losing 14 points to 4 against Whitehaven. Sharlston gave a good account of themselves in the fourth round at Oldham, but the 'sin binning' of one of their players in the first half gave Oldham a numerical advantage that they capitalised on. In the end the professional club's greater experience saw them home by 24 points to 4. Dudley Hill, after their heroics at Keighley, came down to earth with a bump when they lost by 76 points to 14 at Batley. Dudley Hill had switched the tie to the Batley ground but were not rewarded with a good attendance as only 890 spectators witnessed a very one-sided game.

There had been many changes to the structure and format of the Challenge Cup over the past ten years, far more than had happened over the previous ninety. The inclusion of an increased number of amateur clubs in the Cup rather than a qualifying competition was the first major change. That was followed by the inclusion of clubs from France and Russia, Services teams, University teams and clubs from the Rugby League Conference, the summer competition supported by the RFL. Many different types of seeding were tried in an attempt to ensure the number of one-sided games was minimised. The seeding between 1994 and 2004 could have been judged as a qualified success. There were games every year where the winning score exceeded fifty points and rugby league is a sport where that can happen, even at the highest level. Once a team takes control of a game and is physically dominating the opposition, big scores are usually the consequence. However, although there were big scores when amateurs met professionals, there were also many competitive games and a much greater number of shock results than had ever occurred before. Some of the amateur club victories in the third round could be explained by the timing of the games. Playing a professional club in the Challenge Cup, either before that club had begun its league season or when it had perhaps played just one or two competitive games, was certainly a major reason for some of the upsets. However, what also must be considered is the fact that standards in the amateur game had risen. The improved facilities at many amateur clubs attracted more players to the sport, and the consistently tough competition on the field provided by leagues like the NCL did improve those players. Another important factor for many of the professional clubs, playing at the levels below Super League, was the lack of financial stability. Declining attendances and income from all sources often meant that some of the struggling professional clubs were unable to retain and recruit the players they needed to be competitive. The close season was a very difficult time for some of those clubs as it was period when there was virtually no income. Attracting new players to a club in financial difficulties was very hard. A club concentrating on trying to resolve its financial problems was often under prepared for the new season. If that club drew a top amateur outfit in the Cup, before those financial issues had been resolved, then a giant killing act could be on the cards.

After all the changes to the structure and format of the Cup over the past ten years, there was one more major change to be made in time for the start of the 2005 Challenge Cup.

Chapter 9

A Chasm Begins to Open

The major change that took place in time for the start of the 2005 Challenge Cup was when the competition began and ended. In 1897, when the first Challenge Cup was played, it was an end of season competition. However, as it developed the Cup began to be played in the second half of the league season, with the qualifying rounds taking place before Christmas. As the Twentieth Century progressed, the early rounds usually took place in January or February with the final at the end of April or early in May. In 1996 when the professional game moved into the summer, the Challenge Cup remained in its traditional place in the calendar and, because the final was still played in May, some people felt that it was losing its status as the premier knockout competition in rugby league. The successful clubs, in the early part of the season, were sometimes not the ones that contested the end of season play offs. Concerns were also raised, that because it was played in the place in the rugby league calendar formally occupied by the John Player/ Regal Trophy, the Challenge Cup was beginning to be seen, by some of the leading clubs as much less important than the league programme. This concern was perhaps reflected in the decline in Cup attendances in all the rounds prior to the final. In a bid to help to revive interest in the competition, the final was moved to late August where it would, it was hoped, be seen as one of the highlights of the year, as it had been when the professional clubs played in winter and the final was held towards the end of the season. The other effect on the competition from moving the final to August was that the early rounds, that involved professional clubs, could begin later. This move would perhaps mean a 'levelling of the playing field' as the professional league season would be in full swing when the early rounds of the Cup were played. Would this mean the end of the giant killers? The advantage the amateur clubs had of playing underprepared professional teams had gone. If this had been the main factor the amateurs had in their favour between 1996 and 2004 when they played professional clubs, then perhaps giant killing acts could be consigned to the history books.

The majority of results in 2005 seemed to confirm the view that now the amateurs had lost their advantage, the gap in skills and ability would be as wide as ever and would probably continue to get wider. This was the year that Rochdale Hornets beat Illingworth by 120 points to 4, Halifax scored 76 unanswered points against Lock Lane, and Castleford beat Hull Dockers by 72 points to 4. Added to these were another four ties where the professionals scored fifty or more points but then came some unexpected results. Sheffield Eagles played Waterhead, at Castleton Gabriels soccer ground, and were very lucky to win by 22 points to 16. Wath Brow Hornets, however, went one better when they played Dewsbury at Whitehaven and won by 30 points to 28. Wath Brow were leading by 24 points to 12 at half time and added to the lead just after the interval when forward Scott Teare crashed over. At 30 points to 12 Wath Brow looked to be coasting into the next round, but then Dewsbury began a fight back that saw them level the scores at 30 points all. Wath Brow's Gavin Curwen won the game for the amateurs when he kicked a penalty in the 61st minute and, although Dewsbury continued to press the Wath Brow line, the Cumbrians managed to defend their lead. Wath Brow's reward was a trip to the South of France to play Toulouse. Wath Brow will have enjoyed the experience but not the 60 points to 12 defeat they suffered at the hands of a club that made history that year by becoming the first from France to reach the semi-finals of the Challenge Cup. The attendances in the third round games in 2005 were very disappointing. Only two ties attracted four figure attendances, 3,341 at Castleford when they entertained Hull Dockers and 1,750 at Hull KR for their game against Siddal. The rest of the attendances will hardly have covered the home club's expenses in staging the game.

Workington dejection – Thornhill Trojans v Workington Town 2006

The 2006 third round produced big scores by two professional clubs. Dewsbury and Hull KR both ran in over sixty points but the majority of ties were competitive and, for the third time since 1998, Workington were beaten by amateur opposition. Thornhill Trojans were the giant killers in 2006 following their narrow 16 points to 12 victory over the Cumbrians at Dewsbury's ground. Workington had taken an early lead but then a try, conversion and a penalty from full back Craig Holmes gave Thornhill a lead that they did not surrender. Workington came back strongly in the second half but another penalty from Holmes, seven minutes from time, sealed the win. The giant killers were, for the second year running, rewarded for their success with a trip to Southern France. Unfortunately, Super League club Catalan Dragons were far too strong for Thornhill, scoring sixty six unanswered points in an easy victory. However, like Wath Brow Hornets the previous season, Thornhill will no doubt have enjoyed their visit to France.

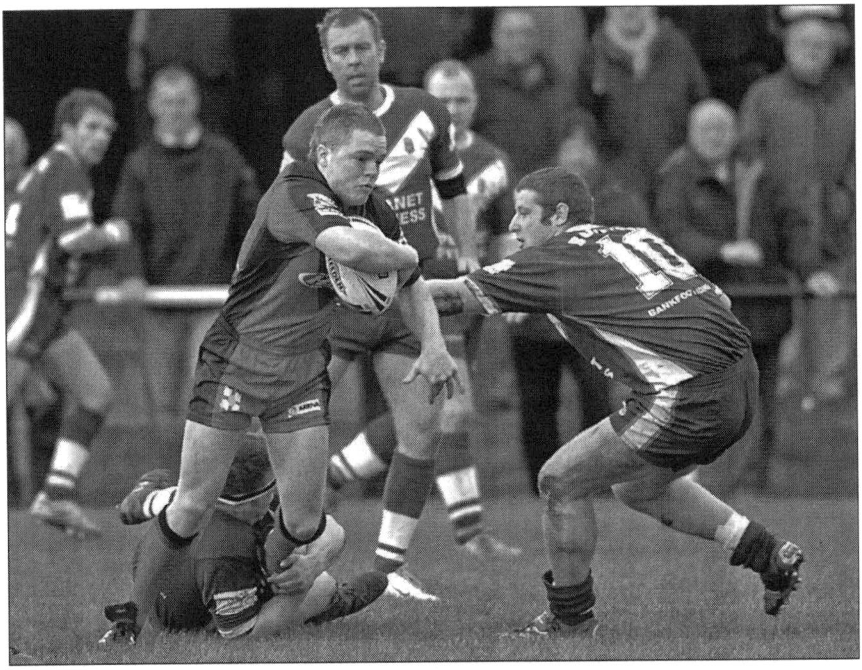

West Bowling v London Skolars 2007

The 2007 Challenge Cup did not produce any giant killers, the first blank year since 2002. Workington Town's 18 points to 10 victory over Oulton was the closest contest and although Oulton battered the Workington line in a frantic last ten minutes, they could not find a way through. London Skolars beat West Bowling by 24 points to 8 in a game that had to be played at Halifax rugby union club because West Bowling's home ground did not have any cover for spectators. London Skolars led the Bradford amateurs by 6 points to 4 at half time and, added three more converted tries to seal a fairly comfortable victory. East Hull, in a tie staged at Hull Ionians rugby union club, were leading Oldham late in the second half when two tries from winger Alex Wilkinson swung the game in the professional club's favour. Apart from those three games the rest of the ties were very one-sided. Both Halifax and Castleford scored over eighty points, Widnes scored seventy eight and Batley scored sixty signalling that perhaps the gap between amateurs and professionals was now beginning to resemble a chasm. The third round in the 2008 competition appeared to confirm that view. Only London Skolars 20 points to 8 victory over Leeds amateurs Queens was a close game. Queens led by 8 points to 4 at half time but then had a player sin binned just after the interval and Skolars capitalised upon their numerical advantage to establish an unassailable lead. The rest of the ties, judging by the scores, were very one-sided. Leeds Metropolitan University became the first student team to reach the third round but they could not compete against Doncaster, losing by 44 points to 10.

In 2009 ten amateur clubs were involved in the third round. There were two close results. Swinton beat Siddal, scraping home by 10 points to 6. Hunslet travelled to Whitehaven's Recreation ground to play Kells and were able to defend their 18 points to nil half time lead against a determined fight back by the Cumbrians. Kells actually won the second half by 12 points to 4 but the points they conceded in the first half proved decisive, and by winning 22 points to 12 Hunslet progressed to the next round. Over the one hundred plus years that the Challenge

Leeds Metropolitan University v Doncaster 2008

Cup has been played the junior/amateur clubs had often been written off as not providing a real challenge when they faced senior/professional opposition. After the 2007 and 2008 competitions I am sure there were many commentators on the sport that supported that view. One-sided games and disappointing attendances must have made many people question the value of having amateurs involved in the Challenge Cup, so what happened in Cumbria on the 8th March 2009 possibly came as something of a surprise. London Skolars were having a difficult time in Championship One, and had in fact won only one game all season. However, because of what had happened in the 2007 and 2008 competitions when the amateurs played professionals, very few people could have expected that Wath Brown Hornets would become giant killers for the third time when they beat London Skolars by 14 points to 12. In front of only 320 spectators, Wath Brow were behind by 12 points to nil with seconds to go in the first half when they were awarded a penalty. Ryan Robb kicked the goal that at the end of the game was to prove decisive. Wath Brow fought back strongly in the second half and took the lead in the 69th minute when Scott Teare scored under the posts leaving Ryan Robb with an easy conversion to seal the win. Wath Brow drew Featherstone Rovers, in the fourth round, and although they competed for the full eighty minutes the Cumbrians were no match for the Championship club losing by 54 points to 16. The 2009 Challenge Cup, as well as producing giant killers, was also marred by controversy. The Doncaster versus Queens tie played at Doncaster's Keepmoat Stadium was abandoned after sixty one minutes because of crowd trouble. This was the first time for seventy years that a rugby league match involving a professional club had been abandoned for crowd trouble. An RFL investigation took place after the match. As a result of the investigation the tie was awarded to Doncaster and Queens were thrown out of the competition.

Doncaster, after the controversy of the abandoned match the previous season, became the victims of a giant killing act in 2010 when they lost by 26 points to 0 against Siddal. Doncaster had been in serious financial difficulties and had problems early in the 2010 season, in getting a competitive team on the field. Siddal led by 10 points to nil at half time and, despite a Doncaster fight back, tremendous defence kept the professionals at bay while Siddal added to their score to record the biggest winning margin by a junior/amateur club over professional opposition in the Challenge Cup. In the fourth round Siddal played Batley, at Halifax's ground, and although they lost by 34 points to 2, they were not disgraced. Eight other amateur clubs were involved in round three in 2010, with only Warrington Wizards coming close to providing a shock result when the lost to Swinton by 34 points to 22. The Wizards finished the game stronger and scored three tries in five minutes, close to the end. Swinton, who had been reduced to twelve men just before half time when one of their players was sent off, managed to hold on.

There were no shocks in the 2011 competition. Doncaster did not make any mistakes at home to Thatto Heath winning by 34 points to 22, although the St Helens amateurs put up great deal of resistance and deserved the 22 points they scored. The only other close game took place at Oldham where the home club beat Hunslet Warriors by 28 points to 16. With the scores tied at 16 -16 in the middle of the second half a shock result did look possible, but then the Warriors conceded a penalty followed shortly by a converted try and Oldham had established a winning lead. Unfortunately, 2011 competition might not have produced any giant killers but it did produce the biggest ever win in the Challenge Cup when York beat Northumbria University by 132 points to nil. Chris Thorman, the York stand-off, also created a record with a personal haul of fifty six points

Chris Thorman – York

made up of four tries and twenty goals. The students battled gamely but were totally outclassed. Northumbria University had got through to the third round by beating two other student teams, the University of Central Lancashire in the first round, and Loughborough University in the second round. If they had played one of the stronger amateur teams in the earlier rounds perhaps they would not have reached the third round and been totally out of their depth against a professional club.

Two of the Championship One clubs, Gateshead and South Wales Scorpions, had very difficult tasks in attempting to qualify for the next round of the 2012 competition. When South Wales Scorpions were drawn away to Wath Brow Hornets they will have expected a very tough game and were not disappointed. The Welsh club did not take a winning lead until the 67th minute after wiping out a Wath Brow 18 points to 16 interval lead to get their noses in front, only to be pegged back again by the Cumbrians. The winning try scored by debutant Greg Callow gave the professionals a two point cushion that they managed to defend for the closing minutes of the game to win the tie by 24 points to 22. Gateshead played York Acorn at home with the 28 points to 20 score reflecting just how difficult the professional club found it to subdue their amateur opponents. It took a Joe Brown try ten minutes from time to finally ensure that Gateshead were able to progress into the next round. The only other close game involved a Cumbrian club when Egremont lost by 22 points to 14 to Oldham in a tie played at Whitehaven's ground. The rest of the third round games produced some big scores from the professional clubs, with Halifax's 94 points to 4 victory over Hull amateurs Myton Warriors the largest.

The 2013 competition was the first year that many of the leading amateur clubs were involved in the Challenge Cup after moving their playing season into the summer. The qualifying rounds of the 2013 Cup were played at the end of the 2012 summer season and involved forty amateur clubs including the NCL first and second division clubs. The fourteen NCL Premier Division clubs joined the competition at the second round stage which was played on the 9th March 2013. The eleven amateur clubs that made it through to the third round were joined in the draw by the twenty three Championship clubs and Toulouse Olympique and AS Carcassonne from the French League.

The third round did not produce any giant killers but when Blackbrook led York City Knights by 24 points to 20 with three minutes left to play, it looked as if York were going to be the victims of a giant killing act for the third time in their history. Gary Thornton, the York coach, was a relieved man when he described the last play of the game, that saw full back Tom Carr score a try that he converted to win the tie, as a '*get out of jail card*'. Blackbrook came the closest of the amateur clubs to progressing to the fourth round but, as often happens when amateurs meet professionals; the early lead by the amateur club is then overtaken late in the second half. Leigh Miners Rangers led Barrow 12 points to 6 at half time, but could not add to their twelve points in the second half as twenty two unanswered points saw the Cumbrians progress into the fourth round by 28 points to 12. The University of Gloucestershire All Golds, one of the new Championship One clubs, were also behind by 16 points to 10 at half time in their tie against Skirlaugh. However, in the second half, once winger James Gahan had raced 95 metres to score in the corner the All Golds could breathe more easily adding to that score late in the game to win the tie by 26 points to 16. Unfortunately, as has often happened in the Cup, there were also some very one sided games. Sheffield Eagles beat Leigh East by 112 points to 6; North Wales Crusaders put West Hull to the sword winning by 82 points to 6, while Featherstone Rovers had scored 44 points by half time against Thatto Heath easing off slightly in the second half to win by 76 points to 6. Sheffield and Featherstone fielded strong sides and as both clubs were riding high in the Championship the big scores were not altogether unexpected. None of the amateur clubs staged a tie on their own ground but three rugby union grounds were used to host professional opposition. Siddal played Keighley at Huddersfield YMCA, Ince Rose Bridge used Wigan Rugby Union club for their tie against Hemel Stags, and Skirlaugh entertained The University of Gloucestershire All Golds at Hull Rugby Union club. As Huddersfield YMCA and Hull Rugby Union club already stage Super League Academy games obtaining RFL permission to use the grounds for Challenge Cup ties was presumably

Action from Skirlaugh v The University of Gloucestershire All Golds 2013

relatively straightforward. Very few of the amateur versus professional clashes managed to attract more than 500 spectators, with the 824 recorded for the Barrow against Leigh Miners Rangers game being the highest attendance.

It is impossible to ignore the feeling that perhaps the third round is now viewed by many people in the sport as a preliminary round, with the serious Challenge Cup action starting when the Super League clubs join the competition in the fourth round. Whether that view is correct or not is difficult to confirm. However, what is clear is that, apart from in local newspapers and on local radio very little mention was made of the fact that the Challenge Cup had reached the third round stage. Would the interest in, and attendances at, third round games have increased if more money had been spent on promoting the ties? With a full round of Super League matches taking place over the weekend it was always going to be hard, irrespective of the size of the promotional budget, to persuade the Super League supporter to abandon his or her club in order to watch a third round Challenge Cup game. There were just 260 spectators watching Skirlaugh play the All Golds, but the attendance isn't really surprising as both Hull FC and Hull Kingston Rovers were also playing at home on the same day. Perhaps it is fixture scheduling rather than promoting the games that needs to be addressed if we want to increase the profile of the third round. Or do we have to recognise that in 2013 the Rugby League Challenge Cup is still an important competition but unfortunately, particularly in the early rounds, is no longer able to attract the interest and attendances that it once did?

Chapter 10

Conclusion

If I had written this book twenty years ago I may well have described the Challenge Cup Final as the most important day in the rugby league calendar. However, to many modern day supporters the Super League Grand Final is now arguably a bigger occasion. This is probably a result of a number of factors, one of which could be the financial pressure on fans. For many the traditional trip to Wembley to watch the Cup Final, just a few weeks before the Super League Grand Final, presents a difficult choice. Restricted spending power might prohibit supporters from attending both finals. Because the Super league Grand Final takes place in Manchester, it is obviously cheaper for Northern based supporters to travel to the game. Therefore, unless their club is playing in the Challenge Cup Final, and probably mainly for financial reasons, it is likely that the rugby league supporter will choose to attend the Super League Grand Final. The success of Super League and the focus of the media on the importance of the league and play off games could also have had an impact on how supporters view the Challenge Cup. I believe these are two of the main factors that may have contributed to the fall in status of the Challenge Cup Final. However, despite seeming to lose its kudos as the biggest day in the rugby league calendar, the final still remains very important to the many people who are interested and involved in rugby league. Is that the case with the competition as a whole?

When the Challenge Cup began in 1896 and all the games took place after the league fixtures had been played, the early pioneers of the sport may well have seen an opportunity to promote the final as the pinnacle of the season. According to the quote from the Leeds Mercury that appears in Les Hoole's book 'The Challenge Cup – An Illustrated History', the first final held on the 24th April 1897 at Headingley was, '*A big success, financially, socially and from a football point of view*'. The success was obviously reflected over the years in the rise in the attendances and status of the competition that resulted in the final moving to Wembley in 1929. Even today, despite its perceived decline in importance, the Challenge Cup Final still attracts an impressive attendance. But I do wonder how important to supporters are the Challenge Cup games leading up to the final.

Over recent years, concerns have been expressed about the decline in interest in the early rounds. Changes have been made to the structure and format of the competition and more recently there have been attempts to increase attendances by using special promotions involving offers to season ticket holders, reduced prices and increased advertising. The 'jury is out' on whether these changes are actually helping to revive interest in the Cup. People talk about 'the magic and romance of the Cup' without perhaps understanding what the phrase means to rugby league supporters. For some it could be the final that produces the 'magic and romance'; for others, when an unexpected result happens in the early rounds or when a little club faces a big club in a David versus Goliath encounter. If there is 'magic and romance' in the early rounds, rugby league must have missed many opportunities since 1896 to develop the Challenge Cup into a competition that created this sparkle every season. The one-sided games that occurred in the early years and continue through to today do not help to generate interest. It may be that it is never going to be possible to 'level the playing field' in order to eradicate the '*hack games*', as they were described in the late 1890s. However, I do believe that the Northern Union and later RFL bye law that allowed clubs drawn at home in the Cup to switch the tie to their opponents ground contributed to reducing interest and the opportunity for more giant killing acts to occur. Playing on your home ground with your supporters massed around the touchlines could well have given a junior club the additional advantage they needed to defeat senior opponents. The fact that early in the history of the Cup it became accepted practice for the juniors, if drawn at home, to concede that advantage did devalue the competition. In my opinion, if the only reason that a junior club entered the Cup was to make money, the sport would gain little. Since the Safety in Sports Grounds Act, it has been much more difficult, for today's amateur clubs to stage a cup tie on their own ground. However, it is interesting to speculate why in earlier years more junior clubs didn't give themselves the added advantage, if drawn at home, of playing on their own ground. More victories by junior clubs over senior opposition in the infancy of the competition may have convinced the decision makers to re-structure the Cup in order that more rather than less aspiring junior clubs could challenge senior opponents.

In the early years, it did appear that the competition was inclusive and not just for those clubs that could be described as senior. The concerns in the early years regarding one-sided ties meant access to the Cup was reduced for those clubs outside the senior ranks. This resulted in seeding and qualifying rounds becoming the accepted way for the Cup to be organised, structures that continued virtually unchanged for nearly one hundred years. The competition was clearly organised for the senior clubs, and as I have argued throughout this story, it seemed that any club below senior level that was involved was only there to make up the numbers. This situation did not really change until 1994 when many more amateur clubs were given the opportunity to play against professional opposition. It is obviously impossible to know how the Challenge Cup would have developed if what occurred in 1994 had happened ninety years earlier. However, the FA Cup, soccer's equivalent knockout competition, has retained some of its 'magic and romance' in the early rounds. This could be because the competition has always had a tradition of allowing far more non-league clubs into its first round to face league opposition. Attendances in the FA Cup have declined, as has happened in rugby league, but there are giant killers in soccer every year. They add to the excitement of the competition, and when one of the non-league clubs is drawn against a Premier League club it is often that tie that attracts much of the media attention. Rugby league cannot be compared with soccer, both in terms of its popularity and the ability of the 'minnows' to cope with the 'big fish'. However, as happened after 1994 when there are a greater number of 'minnows' involved, there are more opportunities of an upset occurring. Perhaps it was it too late to revive interest in the competition when the new Challenge Cup structure was introduced. Certainly once Super League began and all the clubs involved in that competition became full-time, the gap between those clubs and the rest of the sport increased dramatically. A full-time player has a tremendous physical and skill advantage over a part-time player and an even greater advantage over an amateur. There is an argument that because of the massive gap between full time players and the rest, perhaps the Challenge Cup should be a competition for those clubs below Super League, with the Super League outfits concentrating on league fixtures and the end of season play offs. A knockout competition in any sport must give opportunities to clubs at all levels to achieve success. If the only unpredictable ties are those in the later stages when all the minor clubs have been eliminated, the competition may not be able to generate some of the excitement that is associated with knockout football. When the underdog, a club that could not compete with its opponents in a league situation, gets an opportunity in a 'one off game' and upsets the odds by winning, I would argue that value is added to the competition as a whole.

Someone introduced to rugby league between 1910 and 1994 would have found it difficult to understand the concept of giant killers in the sport. The only clubs that could fit the description were not junior or amateur but the odd struggling senior club that managed to defeat a more successful outfit. A greater number of opportunities for giant killing acts in the early rounds of the Cup could, in my opinion, have added another intriguing dimension to the competition. The finals of knockout competitions can be memorable, but so can games in the early rounds. Perhaps we missed opportunities between 1910 and 1994 to add to those memories and the fascination of the Cup.

I hope that this book has helped to celebrate the rugby league giant killers, and possibly surprised some people with just how many there have been considering the eighty four years when no junior/amateur club beat a senior/professional club in a straight knockout game. The two junior clubs that beat senior opponents in the two legged first rounds in the late 1940s, Sharlston Rovers and Risehow and Gillhead are also rightly celebrated. What a pity that their victories did not allow them to progress to the second round!

What does the future hold for amateur involvement in the Challenge Cup? I assume the amateurs will continue to take part and there may well be giant killers in the future. The inclusion of three new clubs in the Championship could provide an opportunity for one of the leading amateur clubs to beat professional opposition. If that occurs in years to come I hope that it will still be considered a giant killing act and be recognised as such. Rugby league is a challenging sport, and any team that rises to the challenge of defeating opponents operating at a higher level ought to be celebrated as a giant killer.

This has been a journey through aspects of the history of the Challenge Cup that have not been well recorded until now. The clubs and players that have featured in this book have added a great deal to the competition and deserve to be remembered for their significant contribution as well as for 'Making Up The Numbers'.

Appendix 1

Results in the cup ties involving junior/amateur clubs and senior/professional clubs

The junior/amateur club is highlighted

1897			
1st Round			
Castleford	43	**Allerton**	3
Halifax	55	**Stockport Rangers**	5
Holbeck	38	**Latchford Rangers**	3
Hull	9	**Walkden**	0
Hunslet	75	**Broughton Recreation**	5
Leeds	11	**Rochdale St Clements**	0
Leeds Parish Church	42	**Runcorn Recreation**	0
Manningham	31	**Dukinfield**	3
Rochdale Hornets	63	**Waterhead Hornets**	3
Runcorn	65	**Warrington Locos**	0
St Helens	58	**Lees**	0
Salford	28	**Warrington St Mary's**	0
Widnes	55	**Atherton Hornets**	0
Wigan	3	**Radcliffe**	0
2nd Round			
Bradford	68	**Swinton Church**	3
Crompton	26	**Bradford Church Hill**	0
Eastmoor	3	Stockport	3

Replay			
Stockport	28	**Eastmoor**	8
Rochdale Hornets	8	**St Helens Recreation**	0
Runcorn	52	**Thornton Rangers**	4
Salford	30	**Werneth**	0
3rd Round			
Halifax	50	**Crompton**	0

1898			
1st Round			
Halifax	17	**St Helens Recreation**	0
Hull KR	46	**Hull Marlborough**	0
Hunslet	8	**Lancaster**	3
Salford	9	**Millom**	2
Ulverston	2	Runcorn	19
2nd Round			
Batley	8	**Walkden**	0
Birkenhead Wanderers	0	Bradford	5
Castleford	14	**Whitworth**	7
Huddersfield	14	**Barrow**	6
Hull	18	**Radcliffe**	0
Hull KR	11	**Morley**	0
Leigh	59	**Abbey Hills**	0
Salford	65	**Lees**	2
3rd Round			
Altringham	0	Salford	16
Barton	3	Bramley	9
1899			
1st Round			
Batley	38	**Rochdale Athletic**	0
Broughton Rangers	59	**Rothwell**	8
Holbeck	9	**Birkenhead Wanderers**	3
Huddersfield	43	**Saddleworth Rangers**	2
Hull	21	**Featherstone Rovers**	0
Hunslet	11	**Maryport**	2
Leeds Parish Church	11	**Idle**	0
Morecambe	30	**Latchford Rangers**	0
Oldham	63	**Goole**	0
Rochdale Hornets	28	**Dalton**	0

Runcorn	77	**Runcorn Recreation**	0
St Helens	12	**Whitworth**	3
Salford	63	**Luddendenfoot**	3
Swinton	40	**Fletcher, Russell & Co**	5
Warrington	12	**Barrow**	2
Widnes	48	**Fleetwood**	3
Wigan	28	**Groves United**	3
2nd Round			
Hull	21	**Millom**	0
Normanton	7	Holbeck	2
Outwood Church	0	Leeds Parish Church	6
Salford	31	**Werneth**	0
3rd Round			
Huddersfield	23	**Normanton**	2
Hull	86	**Elland**	0
1900			
1st Round			
Brighouse Rangers	16	**Todmorden**	5
Broughton Rangers	22	**Lancaster**	7
Halifax	19	**Featherstone Rovers**	2
Huddersfield	22	**Idle**	0
Hull	52	**Wath Brow**	0
Leeds Parish Church	5	**Seaton**	0
Normanton	5	Leeds	0
Runcorn	42	**Birstall**	0
Swinton	53	**Eastmoor**	0
Tydlesley	12	**Brookland Rovers**	0
Wakefield Trinity	15	**Hebden Bridge**	0
Windhill	0	Rochdale Hornets	11
2nd Round			
Bradford	12	**Ossett**	0

Huddersfield	13	**Workington**	0
Leeds Parish Church	15	**Altringham**	3
Normanton	0	Batley	3
Runcorn	12	**Maryport**	0
Warrington	44	**Goole**	0
3rd Round			
Stockport	24	**Radcliffe**	3
1901			
1st Round			
Birkenhead Wanderers	2	Millom	0
Dewsbury	9	**Featherstone Rovers**	5
Goole	2	St Helens	12
Hunslet	8	**Wath Brow**	0
Keighley	13	**Kinsley**	0
Leeds Parish Church	11	**Radcliffe**	0
Leigh	38	**Alverthorpe**	0
Liversedge	3	**Normanton**	2
Oldham	19	**Otley**	0
Outwood Church	2	Holbeck	5
Stockport	13	**Shipley**	2
Wakefield Trinity	28	**Eastmoor**	6
Whitehaven Recreation	0	Widnes	3
2nd Round			
Castleford	3	**Workington**	2
Hebden Bridge	3	Broughton Rangers	33
Hull KR	11	**Maryport**	0
Sowerby Bridge	3	Brighouse Rangers	6
Wakefield	21	**Aspatria**	2
Warrington	19	**Heckmondwike**	2

3rd Round			
Birkenhead Wanderers	2	Widnes	10
1902			
1st Round			
Altringham	12	**Carnforth**	4
Askham	0	Widnes	3
Aspatria	2	Rochdale Hornets	4
Castleford	15	**Hebden Bridge**	7
Holbeck	29	**Alverthorpe**	8
Huddersfield	22	**Kendal Hornets**	0
Hunslet	37	**Wath Brow**	0
Maryport	0	Oldham	27
Otley	0	Leeds	5
Outwood Church	5	Morecambe	5
Replay			
Morecambe	15	**Outwood Church**	0
Salford	28	**Pontefract**	2
South Shields	5	Bradford	23
Werneth	4	Lancaster	6
Windhill	5	Millom	0
2nd Round			
Goole	3	**Kirkstall**	3
Replay			
Kirkstall	0	Goole	3
Leeds	31	**Windhill**	0
3rd Round			
Heckmondwike	7	**Ossett**	4
Swinton	34	**Whitehaven Recreation**	0

1903			
1st Round			
Birkenhead Wanderers	15	**Werneth**	0
Bramley	10	**Pontefract**	5
Castleford	2	**Thrum Hall**	0
Halifax	34	**Salterhebble**	0
Hunslet	18	**Cleckheaton**	5
Keighley	37	**Heckmondwike**	0
Kendal Hornets	3	Morecambe	5
Kinsley	0	Brighouse Rangers	8
Manningham	0	**Idle**	0
Replay			
Idle	0	Manningham	12
Rochdale Hornets	33	**Alverthorpe**	0
Seaton	2	Barrow	5
South Shields	58	**St Pauls**	0
Sowerby Bridge	5	Batley	14
Windhill	0	Normanton	8
2nd Round			
Barrow	15	**Wath Brow**	5
Hull	45	**Hull Marlborough**	0
Hunslet	7	**Outwood Church**	0
York	17	**Otley**	2
1904			
Intermediate Round			
Birkenhead Wanderers	6	**Marsh Hornets**	0
Bramley	15	**Hebden Bridge**	8
Brighouse Rangers	6	**Otley**	0
Dewsbury	18	**Beverley**	10
Holbeck	11	**Outwood Church**	0
Millom	7	**Parton**	8

Rochdale Hornets	28	**Rochdale Athletic**	6
Roose	0	Barrow	34
St Helens	48	**Highfield**	5
1st Round			
Broughton Rangers	26	**Parton**	0
Salford	57	**Brookland Rovers**	0
1905			
Intermediate Round			
Barrow St George's	2	Morecambe	8
Beverley	2	York	9
Huddersfield	20	**Victoria Rangers**	3
Rochdale Hornets	2	**Chadderton**	0
1st Round			
Hull	52	**Leigh Shamrocks**	0
Hull KR	73	**Brookland Rovers**	5
Hunslet	22	**Parton**	3
Leeds	20	**Ossett**	0
1906			
1st Round			
Keighley	13	**Egremont**	0
Victoria Rangers	0	Widnes	0
Replay			
Widnes	5	**Victoria Rangers**	3
2nd Round			
Featherstone Rovers	23	Widnes	2
Salford	38	**Egerton**	5
3rd Round			
Keighley	3	**Featherstone Rovers**	0
1907			
Intermediate Round			
Barrow	24	**Pemberton**	0

Newington Rovers	3	York	3
Replay			
York	14	**Newington Rovers**	5
Saville Green	10	Bramley	0
1st Round			
Huddersfield	38	**Brighouse St James**	0
Keighley	18	**Brookland Rovers**	0
Radcliffe Rangers	0	York	13
Workington	3	Wakefield Trinity	3
Replay			
Wakefield Trinity	16	**Workington**	5
2nd Round			
Whitehaven Recreation	0	Keighley	14
1908			
1st Round			
Barrow	28	**Millom**	5
Batley	32	**Barrow St George's**	5
Beverley	3	Merthyr Tydfil	15
Half Acre Trinity	2	York	7
Whitehaven Recreation	13	St Helens	8
Wigan Highfield	3	Bramley	3
Replay			
Bramley	8	**Wigan Highfield**	6
2nd Round			
Merthyr Tydfil	33	**Whitehaven Recreation**	5
1909			
Barrow	36	**Barrow St George**	0
Beverley	7	Ebbw Vale	2
Normanton	10	Hull	20
Runcorn	23	**Egremont**	5
Pemberton	6	Keighley	41

2nd Round			
Halifax	53	**Beverley**	2
1910			
1st Round			
Purston White Horse	10	Halifax	23
Salford	64	**York Irish National League**	0
Warrington	31	**Wigan Highfield**	3
2nd Round			
Warrington	37	**Millom**	0
1911			
1st Round			
Broughton Moor	6	Runcorn	23
Dewsbury	47	**York Grove United**	0
Normanton St John's	6	Broughton Rangers	10
Pemberton	4	Bradford Northern	12
Widnes	23	**Lane End United**	0
1912			
1st Round			
Beverley	5	Hull KR	34
Dewsbury	36	**Lane End United**	9
Millom	0	Keighley	11
Normanton St John's	6	Warrington	6
Replay			
Warrington	75	**Normanton St John's**	0
Wigan	35	**Wigan Highfield**	10
1913			
1st Round			
Bradford Northern	33	**Pemberton**	4
Broughton Rangers	59	**Barton**	0
Elland	2	Wakefield Trinity	15

Hull	24	**Seaton**	2
Normanton St John's	4	Oldham	17
Rochdale Hornets	15	**Featherstone Rovers**	3
1914			
1st Round			
Huddersfield	119	**Swinton Park**	2
Hull KR	62	**Millom**	0
St Helens	27	**Wigan Highfield**	4
York	45	**Glasson Rangers**	0
2nd Round			
Featherstone Rovers	3	Hull	27
1915			
1st Round			
Brighouse Rangers	0	Salford	26
Featherstone Rovers	0	St Helens	6
Keighley	8	**Askham**	5
Widnes	13	**St Helens Recreation**	4
Wigan Highfield	0	Swinton	2
2nd Round			
Rochdale Hornets	75	**Broughton Moor**	13
1920			
1st Round			
Bramley	13	**Wigan Highfield**	0
Halifax	55	**Brookland Rovers**	0
Featherstone Rovers	2	Broughton Rangers	17
Hull	75	**BOCM**	2
Leeds	44	**Millom**	5
Warrington	9	**Askham in Furness**	0
Wigan	64	**Healey Street Adults**	3

1921			
1st Round			
Askham	2	Bradford Northern	7
Oldham	41	**Elland Wanderers**	5
Swinton	25	**BOCM**	5
Widnes	41	**Dearham Wanderers**	5
Wigan Highfield	10	Broughton	15
2nd Round			
Featherstone Rovers	0	Dewsbury	22
1922			
1st Round			
Elland Wanderers	0	Oldham	29
Rochdale Hornets	54	**Broughton Moor**	2
Swinton	24	**BOCM**	5
Widnes	5	**Wigan Highfield**	5
Replay			
Wigan Highfield	4	Widnes	9
2nd Round			
Keighley	15	**Askham**	0
1923			
1st Round			
Norwood	3	St Helens	29
Wakefield Trinity	67	**Hensingham**	13
Salford	16	**Castleford**	0
Wigan Highfield	16	**Cadishead and Irlam**	0
York	40	**Millom**	0
1924			
1st Round			
Barrow	67	**Dearham Wanderers**	3
Broughton Rangers	34	**Hull St Patrick's**	0
Hull KR	24	**Castleford**	2

Wardley	0	St Helens	73
Warrington	46	**Dalton**	3
1925			
1st Round			
Hunslet	25	**Castleford**	0
Leeds	27	**Twelve Apostles**	0
Wigan	116	**Flimby and Fothergill**	0
2nd Round			
St Helens Recreation	74	**Dalton**	5
1926			
1st Round			
Barrow	44	**Barrow Cambridge Street**	0
Castleford	12	St Helens Recreation	18
Hensingham	0	Huddersfield	33
Hull	27	**Pemberton**	3
Hull KR	28	**Barnsley United**	0
1927			
1st Round			
Batley	32	**Cottingham**	5
Dewsbury	20	**Dearham Wanderers**	5
Wigan	51	**Pemberton**	11
1928			
1st Round			
Batley	31	**Cottingham**	2
Bradford Northern	17	**Twelve Apostles**	0
Warrington	43	**Kinsley**	2
Whitehaven Recreation	0	Swinton	44
1929			
1st Round			
Castleford	31	**Whitehaven Recreation**	7
Dewsbury	37	**Cottingham**	0

St Helens	32	**Lindley**	2
Wigan Highfield	45	**Uno's Dabs**	0
1930			
1st Round			
Halifax	74	**Featherstone Juniors**	9
Hull	44	**Bickershaw Hornets**	10
Keighley	6	**Great Clifton**	5
Leigh	48	**Cottingham**	0
1931			
1st Round			
Bramley	7	**Golden Lions**	3
Huddersfield	60	**Brookland Rovers**	2
Lindley	2	Rochdale	13
Wigan Highfield	41	**Featherstone Juniors**	3
1932			
1st Round			
Barrow	65	**Lindley**	5
Dewsbury	27	**Uno's Dabs**	10
Great Clifton	2	Broughton Rangers	20
1933			
1st Round			
Askern Welfare	0	Wigan	46
Halifax	42	**Uno's Dabs**	5
Hull	37	**Higginshaw**	9
York	35	**Barrow Marsh Hornets**	6
1934			
1st Round			
Bramley	20	**Dearham Wanderers**	11
Hull KR	18	**Wigan Rangers**	2
London Highfield	32	**Hull St Mary's**	2
St Helens Recreation	32	**Pendlebury Juniors**	3

1935			
1st Round			
Barrow	28	**Sharlston Red Rose**	3
Castleford	33	**Astley and Tyldesley Colliery**	4
Manchester Ship Canal	9	Dewsbury	28
Rochdale Hornets	28	**Barrow Marsh Hornets**	18
1936			
1st Round			
Leigh	49	**Seaton**	4
Oldham	38	**Higginshaw**	2
1937			
1st Round			
Goole	2	Broughton Rangers	14
Widnes	39	**Higginshaw**	2
1938			
1st Round			
Barrow	83	**Maryport**	3
Rochdale	50	**Glasshoughton**	2
St Helens	39	**Pendlebury Juniors**	0
1939			
1st Round			
Bradford Northern	37	**Seaton**	7
Hunslet	48	**United Glass Blowers**	5
Sharlston Red Rose	5	Bramley	23
Swinton	46	**Higginshaw**	3
1946			
1st Round			
1st leg			
Higher Ince	3	Widnes	30
Hull Juniors	0	Bramley	29
Hull KR	18	**Langworthy Juniors**	0

Kells	0	Warrington	3
Sharlston Rovers	12	Workington Town	7
2nd leg			
Widnes	42	**Higher Ince**	3
Bramley	51	**Hull Juniors**	3
Langworthy Juniors	7	Hull KR	14
Warrington	27	**Kells**	0
Workington Town	16	**Sharlston Rovers**	2
1947			
1st Round			
1st leg			
Liverpool Stanley	27	**Pemberton Rovers**	6
Warrington	46	**Brookland Rovers**	3
Wheldale Colliery	0	Halifax	25
Workington Town	48	**Widnes Dragons**	0
2nd leg			
Pemberton Rovers	5	Liverpool Stanley	20
Brookland Rovers	3	Warrington	32
Halifax	20	**Wheldale Colliery**	10
Widnes Dragons	5	Workington Town	21
1948			
1st Round			
1st leg			
Bramley	3	**Vine Tavern**	3
Abandoned 43 minutes			
Replay			
Bramley	10	**Vine Tavern**	2
Keighley	11	**Risehow and Gillhead**	0
Rochdale Hornets	13	**Pemberton Rovers**	0
St Helens	48	**Buslingthorpe Vale**	0

2nd leg			
Vine Tavern	6	Bramley	17
Risehow and Gillhead	10	Keighley	2
Pemberton Rovers	0	Rochdale Hornets	11
Buslingthorpe Vale	2	St Helens	13
1949			
1st Round			
1st leg			
Normanton	4	Belle Vue Rangers	9
Oldham	30	**Broughton Moor**	0
Vine Tavern	4	York	11
2nd leg			
Belle Vue Rangers	12	**Normanton**	0
Broughton Moor	2	Oldham	35
York	17	**Vine Tavern**	30
1950			
1st Round			
1st leg			
Cardiff	10	Salford	15
Broughton Moor	5	Wakefield Trinity	28
Worsley Boys Club	7	Hunslet	45
2nd leg			
Salford	20	**Cardiff**	15
Wakefield Trinity	73	**Broughton Moor**	3
Hunslet	18	**Worsley Boys Club**	9
1951			
1st Round			
1st leg			
Batley	41	**Broughton Moor**	3
Leigh	43	**Latchford Albion**	0
Llanelli	9	Barrow	23

2nd leg			
Broughton Moor	0	Batley	36
Latchford Albion	0	Leigh	19
Barrow	39	**Llanelli**	5
1952			
1st Round			
1st leg			
Whitehaven	16	**Ryland's Recreation**	0
2nd leg			
Ryland's Recreation	9	Whitehaven	9
1953			
1st Round			
1st leg			
Warrington	46	**Orford Tannery**	2
Widnes	28	**NDLB**	0
2nd leg			
Orford Tannery	8	Warrington	46
NDLB	3	Widnes	22
1954			
1st Round			
1st leg			
Latchford Albion	20	Wigan	40
Wheldale Colliery	6	Workington Town	32
2nd leg			
Wigan	41	**Latchford Albion**	2
Workington Town	50	**Wheldale Colliery**	2
1955			
1st Round			
Workington Town	43	**Dewsbury Celtic**	0

1956			
1st Round			
Keighley	33	**Triangle Valve**	8
Rochdale Hornets	55	**Stanningley**	0
1957			
1st Round			
Barrow	53	**Wakefield Loco**	12
Halifax	48	**Widnes St Maries**	0
1958			
1st Round			
Widnes	51	**Orford Tannery**	2
York	50	**Lock Lane**	5
1959			
1st Round			
Hunslet	55	**Kells**	9
York	54	**Astley & Tyldesley Colliery**	2
1960			
2nd Round			
Oldham	55	**Walney Central**	4
1961			
1st Round			
Dewsbury Celtic	0	Castleford	32
Hull KR	56	**Pilkington Recreation**	8
1962			
1st Round			
Brookhouse	4	Doncaster	7
Hunslet	53	**St Anne's**	10
1963			
1st Round			
Liverpool City	11	**Roose**	0
York Imperial	4	Bramley	15

1964			
1st Round			
Featherstone Rovers	60	**Stanningley**	4
2nd Round			
Blackpool Borough	48	**Thames Board Mills**	8
1965			
1st Round			
Blackpool Borough	27	**Crosfields**	4
Swinton	48	**Dewsbury Celtic**	5
1966			
1st Round			
Barrow	11	**Crosfields**	2
Widnes	23	**Brookhouse**	5
1967			
1st Round			
Blackbrook	12	York	23
BOCM	9	Liverpool City	20
1968			
1st Round			
Castleford	39	**BOCM**	6
Halifax	24	**Leigh Miners Welfare**	7
1969			
1st Round			
Wakefield	50	**Ackworth**	7
Wigan	61	**Leigh Miners Welfare**	0
1970			
1st Round			
Doncaster	22	**Glasson Rangers**	4
Huddersfield	15	**Lock Lane**	10

1971			
1st Round			
Dewsbury	25	**BOCM**	3
Hunslet	49	**Thames Board Mills**	5
1972			
1st Round			
Bramley	19	**Pilkington Recreation**	5
Dewsbury Celtic	2	Featherstone Rovers	34
1973			
1st Round			
Leigh	27	**Dewsbury Celtic**	4
Millom	5	Hunslet	18
1974			
1st Round			
Leigh	63	**Kippax White Swan**	7
Wigan	37	**Lock Lane**	9
1975			
1st Round			
Dewsbury Celtic	15	Hull KR	31
New Hunslet	9	**Mayfield**	5
1976			
1st Round			
Leigh	37	**Pointer Panthers**	8
Warrington	16	**Leigh Miners Welfare**	12
1977			
1st Round			
Beecroft & Whiteman	2	Swinton	10
Pilkington Recreation	4	Wigan	10

1978			
1st Round			
Dewsbury Celtic	5	Wigan	15
Pilkington Recreation	22	Castleford	23
1979			
1st Round			
Leigh	23	**Leigh Miners Welfare**	10
Oldham	23	**Ace Amateurs**	5
1980			
1st Round			
Ace Amateurs	5	Widnes	22
Hull	33	**Millom**	10
1981			
1st Round			
Pilkington Recreation	7	York	18
1982		**No Junior Clubs**	
1983		**No Junior Clubs**	
1984		**No Junior Clubs**	
1985		**No Junior Clubs**	
1986			
Preliminary Round			
Hull	38	**Dudley Hill**	10
Hunslet	20	**Kells**	8
1987			
Preliminary Round			
Castleford	74	**Blackbrook**	6
Kells	4	Fulham	4
Replay			
Fulham	22	**Kells**	14
1st Round			
Mansfield Marksman	14	**Heworth**	7

1988			
Preliminary Round			
Kells	0	Leeds	28
Leigh Miners Welfare	4	Hunslet	23
1st Round			
Heworth	4	Halifax	60
1989			
Preliminary Round			
Milford	0	Swinton	36
West Hull	2	Doncaster	48
1st Round			
Chorley Borough	8	**Thatto Heath**	4
1990			
Preliminary Round			
Thatto Heath	2	Batley	45
1st Round			
Salford	56	**Bison**	6
1991			
Preliminary Round			
Hensingham	7	Dewsbury	24
Leigh East	12	Bradford Northern	24
Salford	44	**Cutsyke**	4
1992			
1st Round			
Kells	14	Hunslet	32
1993 No Junior Clubs			

1994			
3rd Round			
Batley	58	**Dewsbury Celtic**	2
Barrow	34	**East Leeds**	10
Bramley	46	**Redhill**	20

Carlisle	42	**Askham**	8
Dewsbury	64	**Hensingham**	6
Doncaster	36	**Wigan St Patricks**	4
Highfield	16	**Saddleworth**	13
Huddersfield	42	**Woolston Rovers**	6
Hunslet	58	**Barrow Island**	2
Keighley	68	**Oulton**	0
London Crusaders	40	**Shaw Cross**	14
Rochdale Hornets	32	**Millom**	0
Ryedale York	52	**Leigh Miners Welfare**	2
Swinton	30	**Irlam Hornets**	0
Whitehaven	44	**West Hull**	4
Workington Town	24	**Beverley**	10
1995			
3rd Round			
Barrow	56	**East Leeds**	0
Batley	32	**Shaw Cross**	4
Bramley	42	**Woolston**	2
Carlisle	34	**Dudley Hill**	4
Dewsbury	72	**Kells**	12
Highfield	4	**Beverley**	27
Huddersfield	44	**Wigan St Judes**	10
Hull KR	58	**Thornhill**	6
Hunslet	64	**Wigan St Patricks**	4
Leigh	40	**Heworth**	28
London Broncos	30	**Ellenborough**	10
Rochdale Hornets	48	**Lock Lane**	16
Ryedale York	50	**Barrow Island**	20
Swinton	30	**Millom**	10
Whitehaven	64	**Moorends**	12

4th Round			
Beverley	20	Batley	30
1996			
3rd Round			
Bramley	22	**Heworth**	18
Carlisle	36	**West Bowling**	6
Chorley	12	**Thatto Heath**	27
Highfield	20	**West Hull**	35
Hull KR	44	**Eastmoor**	12
Hunslet	30	**Skirlaugh**	18
Leigh	58	**Egremont**	6
York	30	**Lock Lane**	10
4th Round			
Rochdale	54	**Thatto Heath**	8
West Hull	10	York	6
5th Round			
West Hull	8	Wakefield Trinity	40
1997			
3rd Round			
Barrow	16	**Siddal**	8
Carlisle	34	**BRK**	8
Dewsbury	44	**West Hull**	18
Doncaster	15	**Oulton**	14
Featherstone	48	**Moldgreen**	14
Huddersfield	82	**East Leeds**	0
Hull	42	**Lock Lane**	0
Hull KR	44	**Mayfield**	4
Hunslet	54	**Woolston**	6
Keighley	62	**Redhill**	4
Lancashire Lynx	24	**Hull Dockers**	4
Leigh	68	**Wigan St Patricks**	10

Rochdale Hornets	30	**Walney Central**	6
Wakefield Trinity	52	**Ovenden**	0
Whitehaven	12	**Skirlaugh**	6
Widnes	56	**Clayton**	2
Workington	86	**Thatto Heath**	0
York	14	**Dudley Hill**	21
4th Round			
Carlisle	62	**Dudley Hill**	2
1998			
3rd Round			
Barrow	52	**Farnworth**	8
Batley	44	**Oulton**	2
Bramley	10	**Ellenborough Rangers**	16
Dewsbury	40	**Thornhill**	2
Doncaster	18	**Featherstone Lions**	23
Featherstone	56	**Woolston Rovers**	0
Hull KR	34	**Queens**	16
Hunslet	44	**Skirlaugh**	12
Keighley	66	**Saddleworth**	16
Lancashire Lynx	46	**West Hull**	0
Leigh	44	**Hunslet Warriors**	4
Rochdale Hornets	44	**Leigh Miners Rangers**	4
Swinton	74	**Folly Lane**	6
Wakefield Trinity	44	**BRK**	6
Whitehaven	48	**Lock Lane**	7
Workington	12	**Haydock**	8
York	37	**Norland**	5
4th Round			
Egremont	18	Workington	0
Ellenborough Rangers	14	Hunslet	12
Featherstone Lions	20	Hull KR	56

Ovenden	0	Salford	74
5th Round			
Hull	78	**Ellenborough Rangers**	0
Sheffield Eagles	84	**Egremont**	6
1999			
3rd Round			
Barrow	44	**Dudley Hill**	16
Batley	40	**Lock Lane**	10
Bramley	12	**Leigh Miners Rangers**	18
Dewsbury	38	**Siddal**	10
Doncaster	35	**Oldham St Anne's** After Extra Time	21
Featherstone Rovers	70	**Thornhill**	6
Hull KR	56	**Wath Brow**	4
Hunslet	66	**Townville**	6
Keighley	48	**Mayfield**	2
Lancashire Lynx	50	**Askham**	3
Rochdale Hornets	52	**Wigan St Judes**	12
Swinton	38	**Moldgreen**	4
Whitehaven	22	**Saddleworth**	6
Widnes	34	**West Hull**	4
Workington	30	**Skirlaugh**	4
York	57	**Egremont**	2
Oldham	26	**Eccles**	7
4th Round			
Featherstone Lions	6	Halifax	74
Leigh Miners Rangers	0	Hull KR	52
2000			
3rd Round			
Barrow	42	**Featherstone Lions**	12
Batley	0	**Oldham St Anne's**	10

Lock Lane	16	Villeneuve	26
Dewsbury	66	**Stanley**	0
Featherstone Rovers	64	**Wigan St Patricks**	6
Keighley	90	**Cardiff Cougars**	0
Hull KR	32	**Ideal Isberg**	4
Lancashire Lynx	18	**Walney Central**	6
Leigh	34	**Siddal**	12
Sheffield Eagles	14	**Thornhill**	16
Whitehaven	42	**Shaw Cross**	0
Widnes	76	**West Hull**	8
Workington	12	**Skirlaugh**	2
York	56	**Dudley Hill**	10
Swinton	74	**Waterhead**	1
Oldham	44	**Wigan St Judes**	0
4th Round			
London	44	**Wath Brow**	18
Castleford	64	**Oldham St Anne's**	8
York	56	**Thornhill**	2
2001			
3rd Round			
Halton Simms Cross	10	Villeneuve	42
Dewsbury	48	**Leigh Miners Rangers**	10
Rochdale Hornets	52	**Wigan Rose Bridge**	0
Barrow	40	**Askham**	16
Batley	70	**Heworth**	0
Chorley	8	**Woolston Rovers**	22
Doncaster	44	**Siddal**	14
Featherstone Rovers	56	**Eccles**	0
Gateshead	34	**Wigan St Judes**	20
Sheffield Eagles	42	**East Leeds**	0
Swinton	44	**New Earswick**	12

Whitehaven	34	**Oldham St Anne's**	16
Hunslet	38	**Thornhill**	6
Keighley	76	**Mayfield**	0
Leigh	28	**West Hull**	5
Oldham	64	**Queensbury**	0
Widnes	70	**Wigan St Patricks**	2
Workington Town	38	**Lock Lane**	0
York	24	**Oulton**	12
4th Round			
Warrington	48	**Woolston Rovers**	6
2002			
3rd Round			
Sheffield Eagles	34	**Leigh East**	12
Barrow	28	**Oulton**	5
Lock Lane	14	Doncaster	26
Milford	0	York	42
Wigan St Patricks	4	Dewsbury	28
Woolston Rovers	13	Hunslet	18
Batley	34	**Heworth**	4
Chorley Lynx	10	**Redhill**	2
Halton Simms Cross	12	Leigh	36
Huddersfield	44	**Wath Brow**	4
Oldham	38	**West Hull**	4
Rochdale Hornets	44	**Farnworth**	28
Whitehaven	50	**Dewsbury Celtic**	0
Ellenborough	6	Hull KR	38
Swinton	32	**Skirlaugh** After Extra Time	24
2003			
3rd Round			
Wath Brow	13	Workington	12

Oulton	8	Sheffield Eagles	22
Chorley Lynx	36	**Leigh Miners Rangers**	14
Oldham St Anne's	18	Rochdale Hornets	62
Skirlaugh	8	York	20
Barrow	70	**Embassy**	6
Doncaster	64	**Redhill**	2
Halton Simms Cross	15	London Skolars	8
Hull KR	28	**Siddal**	0
Keighley	33	**Thornhill**	10
Oldham	32	**East Hull**	6
Swinton	46	**Shaw Cross**	0
West Bowling	12	Batley	34
Whitehaven	66	**Cottingham**	6
Woolston Rovers	12	Dewsbury	34
4th Round			
Wath Brow	6	Batley	18
Wigan	82	**Halton Simms Cross**	3
2004			
3rd Round			
Oldham	16	**Castleford Panthers**	8
Sharlston	30	Dewsbury	28
Leigh Miners Rangers	12	Sheffield Eagles	
London Skolars	22	**Mayfield**	16
Hunslet	32	**Featherstone Lions**	0
Ince Rosebridge	8	Batley	42
Crosfields	14	Workington	46
Keighley	14	**Dudley Hill**	16
Doncaster	28	**West Hull**	6
Elland	4	Leigh	64
Featherstone Rovers	96	**Lock Lane**	0
Halifax	66	**Oulton**	10

Swinton	14	**East Hull**	26
Thatto Heath	12	Whitehaven	26
4th Round			
Dudley Hill	14	Batley	76
East Hull	4	Whitehaven	14
Oldham	24	**Sharlston**	4
2005			
3rd Round			
Sharlston	14	Oldham	46
Halifax	76	**Lock Lane**	0
Wath Brow	32	Dewsbury	30
Haydock	4	Hunslet	46
Barrow	42	**East Hull**	22
Castleford	72	**Hull Dockers**	10
Doncaster	54	**Stanningley**	6
York	50	**Elland**	12
Featherstone Rovers	48	**Thornhill**	10
Oldham St Anne's	30	Whitehaven	62
Rochdale	120	**Illingworth**	4
Hull KR	50	**Siddal**	6
Waterhead	16	Sheffield Eagles	22
Workington	44	**Wigan St Judes**	20
4th Round			
Toulouse	60	**Wath Brow**	12
2006			
3rd Round			
Ovenden	10	York	50
Widnes St Maries	14	Barrow	30
Kells	6	Halifax	26
Skirlaugh	14	Featherstone Rovers	36
Oldham	34	**Saddleworth**	10

Dewsbury	68	**Dudley Hill**	0
Hunslet Warriors	0	Widnes	38
East Hull	2	Hunslet	20
Hull KR	62	**York Acorn**	1
Doncaster	34	**Shaw Cross**	18
Thornhill	16	Workington Town	12
Leigh Miners Rangers	6	Rochdale Hornets	34
West Bowling	0	Keighley	34
4th Round			
Catalan Dragons	66	**Thornhill**	0
2007			
3rd Round			
Rochdale Hornets	48	**Saddleworth**	6
West Hull	18	Barrow	70
Leigh Miners Rangers	18	Sheffield Eagles	46
Keighley	34	**Thornhill**	6
Halifax	86	**Eccles**	12
Workington Town	18	**Oulton**	10
Normanton	10	Widnes	78
Castleford	88	**Lock Lane**	10
Batley	60	**Widnes St Maries**	6
Featherstone	52	**Drighlington**	10
Hunslet	40	**Mayfield**	22
West Bowling	8	London Skolars	24
East Hull	10	Oldham	26
2008			
3rd Round			
Rochdale Hornets	50	**York Acorn**	8
Leigh	66	**Featherstone Lions**	0
Batley	42	**East Hull**	10
Widnes	60	**Skirlaugh**	18

Leeds Metropolitan University	16	Doncaster	44
London Skolars	20	**Queens**	8
Wigan St Patricks	14	Workington	50
Wath Brow	14	Swinton	40
Bank Quay	6	Hunslet	36
Oulton	24	Dewsbury	54
Leigh Miners Rangers	14	Whitehaven	40
Salford	66	**Warrington Wizards**	10
2009			
3rd Round			
Kells	12	Hunslet	22
York	50	**Wigan St Patricks**	10
Leeds Metropolitan University	24	Rochdale Hornets	38
Halifax	60	**Loughborough University**	16
Siddal	6	Swinton	10
Wath Brow	14	**London Skolars**	12
Queens's		Doncaster – Abandoned	
Widnes	88	**Saddleworth**	0
Pilkington Recs	24	Batley	34
Oldham	26	**Sharlston**	8
4th Round			
Featherstone Rovers	54	**Wath Brow**	16
2010			
3rd Round			
Widnes	64	**Wigan St Judes**	12
Drighlington	10	Dewsbury	42
Batley	70	**Leeds Metropolitan University**	6
Ovenden	10	Halifax	88

Barrow	62	**Hunslet Warriors**	10
Doncaster	0	**Siddal**	26
Leigh East	14	Hunslet	30
Warrington Wizards	22	Swinton	34
Leigh Miners Rangers	20	Whitehaven	40
4th Round			
Siddal	2	Batley	34
2011			
3rd Round			
Siddal	6	Widnes	54
Oldham	28	**Hunslet Warriors**	16
Batley	64	**Fryston**	10
Sheffield Eagles	82	**Leeds Metropolitan University**	0
Northumbria University	0	York	132
Halifax	76	**Lock Lane**	6
Leigh	68	**Hull Dockers**	24
Milford	16	Gateshead	38
London Skolars	60	**Egremont**	24
Doncaster	34	**Thatto Heath**	22
Leigh Miners Rangers	26	Barrow	56
Swinton	44	**East Hull**	4
Hunslet	48	**Warrington Wizards**	10
2012			
3rd Round			
Dewsbury	84	**Thatto Heath**	12
York	40	**Hull Dockers**	14
Whitehaven	52	**Hunslet Warriors**	6
Myton	4	Halifax	94
Hunslet Old Boys	12	Featherstone Rovers	86
Swinton	66	**Siddal**	0

East Hull	20	Rochdale	40
Dudley Hill	6	Keighley	58
Oulton	8	Sheffield Eagles	58
Gateshead	28	**York Acorn**	20
Doncaster	57	**Sharlston**	10
Wath Brow	22	South Wales Scorpions	24
Egremont	14	Oldham	22
2013			
3rd Round			
Leigh	50	**East Leeds**	4
West Hull	6	North Wales Crusaders	82
Barrow	28	**Leigh Miners Rangers**	12
Blackbrook	24	York City Knights	26
Dewsbury	56	**Myton Warriors**	6
Featherstone Rovers	76	**Thatto Heath**	6
Ince Rose Bridge	4	Hemel Stags	56
Rochdale Hornets	40	**Hunslet Old Boys**	4
Sheffield Eagles	112	**Leigh East**	6
Siddal	14	Keighley	30
Skirlaugh	16	University of Gloucestershire All Golds	26

Appendix 2

Giant Killers

Home Team	Result	Away Team	Year
Normanton	7 - 2	Holbeck	1899
Normanton	5 - 0	Leeds	1900
Birkenhead Wanderers	2 - 0	Millom	1901
Windhill	5 - 0	Millom	1902
Millom	7 - 8	**Parton**	1904
Featherstone Rovers	23 - 2	Widnes	1906
Saville Green	10 - 0	Bramley	1907
Whitehaven Recreation	13 - 8	St Helens	1908
Beverley	7 - 2	Ebbw Vale	1909
Sharlston Rovers	12 - 7	Workington Town (1st leg) Lost 23-14 on aggregate	1946
Risehow & Gillhead	10 - 2	Keighley (2nd leg) Lost 13 – 2 on aggregate	1948
Highfield	4 - 27	**Beverley**	1995
Highfield	20 - 35	**West Hull**	1996
Chorley	12 - 27	**Thatto Heath**	1996
West Hull	10 - 6	York	1996
York	14 - 21	**Dudley Hill**	1997
Bramley	10 - 16	**Ellenborough Rangers**	1998
Doncaster	18 - 23	**Featherstone Lions**	1998
Ellenborough Rangers	14 - 12	Hunslet	1998

Egremont	18 - 0	Workington Town	1998
Bramley	12 - 18	**Leigh Miners Rangers**	1999
Batley	0 - 10	**Oldham St Anne's**	2000
Sheffield Eagles	14 - 16	**Thornhill**	2000
Chorley	8 - 22	**Woolston**	2001
Wath Brow Hornets	13 - 12	Workington Town	2003
Halton Simms Cross	15 - 8	London Skolars	2003
Sharlston Rovers	30 - 28	Dewsbury	2004
Dudley Hill	16 - 14	Keighley	2004
Swinton	14 - 26	**East Hull**	2004
Wath Brow Hornets	32 - 30	Dewsbury	2005
Thornhill	16 - 12	Workington Town	2006
Wath Brow Hornets	14 - 12	London Skolars	2009
Doncaster	0 - 26	**Siddal**	2010

Bibliography

Athletic News
The Yorkshire Post
The Yorkshireman
Leeds Mercury
Huddersfield Examiner
Yorkshire Evening Press
Hull Daily Mail
The Rugby League Challenge Cup- An illustrated history – Les Hoole
The Rugby League Challenge Cup - John Huxley
Code X111
The Dewsbury Reporter
The Wakefield Express
Wigan Observer
The Times and Star
Rugby League Back o' t' wall – The History of Sharlston Rovers by Graham Chalkley
St Helens Reporter
Warrington Guardian
Widnes Weekly News
Goole Times
Gillette Rugby League Yearbook
Rothmans Rugby League Yearbook
Oldham Chronicle

Rugby League Gazette
Barrow Evening Mail
The Western Mail
The Manchester Evening News
Duty and Devotion by James W Bancroft

Other Books by Stuart Sheard

This is the story of a junior rugby union club that, for the majority of its sixty seven years in existence, was called Leeds Chirons. It is a story that reflects some of the changes that have taken place in the sport between 1923 and 1990. If you have ever been involved with 'grassroots' rugby, the events and incidents described in this book will hopefully revive memories of a much simpler time. Leeds Chirons played in an amateur era, when results were important but there were no league tables to worry about.

The game of rugby on a Saturday afternoon and the social activities that followed it were the reasons you played. Some of the memories recounted make it clear just how much impact rugby has on peoples' lives.

Let Them Play By All Means is the story of Yorkshire Rugby Union during World War Two, one of the most difficult times in the lives of many people in Britain, and a largely unrecorded period in the history of rugby union in the County.

Contemporary records, memories, newspaper archives, photographs and documents, help to describe how the sport responded to the life-changing events that took place between 1939 and 1945.

Importantly, the book records how a small group of remarkable club enthusiasts kept the sport going against the odds through the war years, and remembers some of the rugby people who made the ultimate sacrifice.

Available from YPDbooks.com